Rave Reviews for *In the Chat [Room with God]*

"Since we don't spend time in chat rooms (We tri[ed?] using words like 'groovy' and 'psoriasis,' and the Cybe[r...] we found Jedd and Todd's book to be enlightening as well as clever.

"The idea that God would spend time in a chat room with young people like CrossKrys, Blake7, and JennSmiles makes perfect sense. It also makes for a good read. Brush up on your Internet terms and teen vernacular and learn a little about the character of God in the process.

"Read this book."

—Bruce & Stan
Authors of *God Is in the Small Stuff*

"In the Chat Room with God oozes with creativity and the excitement of teens in chat! Great work!

"As people experience the virtual world and strangely hunger for escape and connection, it's refreshing to see how you've allowed God to engage them there. It seems they long to be who they "really are" yet hide behind names and profiles. *In the Chat Room with God* cleverly and gently moves God into the souls of those behind the mask, impacting hearts and lives.

"Reading your book, I felt as if I was again in my teen chat room! The characters are alive and full of spirit.

"Whether readers are experienced in chat rooms or just enjoy a great conversation between friends and God, they will certainly enjoy this book! This would make a great book for a youth drama teams' continued saga over the school-year! Every student and youth worker should crack these pages!"

—Doug Herman
Author of *Faith Quake* and *What Good Is God?*
Speaker, Pure Revolution

"Cool concept, timeless truths, and a profound approach to the big questions of life—presented in a way this generation will listen to and respond."

—Sigmund Brouwer
Author of *The Unrandom Universe: How Science Can Strengthen Your Faith*

"In the Chat Room with God is engaging, thought-provoking, and, well, wow—which happens to be the primary word that kept echoing in my mind as I turned the last page. I read this book in a single sitting, and it not only made me LOL, but even get teary-eyed a time or two. If you're like me, you'll find yourself really growing to care about the teenage characters in this book and the struggles, triumphs, and choices in their lives.

"Best yet, you'll enjoy hooking up with God in a venue that is refreshing and, okay, sure, bizarre—but a lot of fun nevertheless. Perfect to read on your own, with your best friends, or even with a youth group, *In the Chat Room with God* teams a timeless message with a cutting-edge medium, and the result is rich."

—Karen Linamen
Author of *Welcome to the Funny Farm* and *Just Hand Over the Chocolate . . .*

TODD & JEDD HAFER

IN THE
Chat Room
WITH
God

RIVER
OAK
PUBLISHING

Tulsa, Oklahoma

In the Chat Room with God

ISBN 1-58919-970-7
46-275-00001
Copyright © 2002 by Jedd Hafer and Todd Hafer

Published by RiverOak Publishing
P.O. Box 700143
Tulsa, Oklahoma 74170-0143

Dedication

We dedicate this book to the victims of violence
and to their friends and families.

Live in peace with each other.
1 Thessalonians 5:13

"Blessed are the peacemakers,
for they will be called sons of God."
Matthew 5:9

Acknowledgments

The authors want to thank, honor, and generally grovel before the following people . . .

Keith Stubbs and Ron "Buster" Hafer for comedic inspiration.

Pastor Del Hafer (our dad) for biblical insight—and for not killing us when we were teens.

Brennan Manning and Steve Thurman for saying Grace.

Steve Taylor, Nichole Nordeman, D.C. Talk, Ashley Cleveland, Jennifer Knapp, Sara Masen, Sixpence None the Richer, Geoff Moore, and The Choir for songs that have comforted, challenged, inspired, and amazed us.

The teens at Doherty High School, Wasson High School, Colorado Springs Christian School, Woodland Park High School, Southwoods Christian Church, and the Children's Ark for their honesty and graciousness.

Dave Bordon, Jeff Dunn, Debbie Justus, Kelli Portman, and the entire RiverOak staff for courageous, cutting-edge publishing.

Chaplain Pat Cooperrider for showing a Christ-like heart to young people—and not so young people—every day.

Valerie Skaret for showing us how a Christian teen can live purely in an impure world—and still be really cool.

Our siblings, Chadd and Bradd Hafer, for their friendship and brotherhood.

Our wives (one for each of us), Jody and Lindsey Hafer, and our kids for believing in us and enduring deadline pressures and odd-hour writing binges.

Foreword

I have had the great pleasure of knowing Todd and Jedd Hafer since I was about fifteen. I can attest personally that they are great guys from a fantastic family. Funny people. Good-hearted, good-natured, and beyond that, solid Christian people. And while it would be tempting to endorse their new book on the merits of our friendship alone, it would also be irresponsible. I could not and would not in good faith "get behind" this book for the sake of doing friends a favor. That being said, I offer the following:

For many years I have been the first to jump on the "technology is bad" bandwagon. Call it intimidation. Call it misguided conviction. Call it general cluelessness. But in the past couple of years, as the age of technology has given a whole new generation unlimited access to cell phones, pagers, and the Internet, I have actually heard myself say in certain circles, "Well, when I was a teenager, I never would have been allowed to blah blah blah the way kids do today." As if the very invention of chat rooms was somehow directly responsible for a new kind of moral decay among our youth. As if we would all be a lot better off if we simply stuck our heads in the sand and ignored the cyber advances of our culture. It just scared me, I think, and overwhelmed me. And I'm only thirty.

When I began to read *In the Chat Room with God*, I was prepared for something cute. Something quirky and anecdotal. Something far less brave than what I actually encountered. Todd and Jedd Hafer are not only wise enough to recognize that this particular form of communication is highly relevant to teen culture, but they are also courageous enough to discuss the real topics. The big ones. The ones that teens like you talk about for hours in chat rooms. Sex. Suicide. Rage. Friendships. Self-image. Divorce. Forgiveness. Drugs.

And then the bravest part of all—to include God as one of the chat room characters. To imagine what He would say to these kids as they wrestle with their own experiences, their own convictions, and their own apathy. And lest anyone balk at the creative liberty taken in creating dialogue for a cyber-deity, rest assured that this story is packed full of so many biblical principles and relevant references to Scripture that there are no lessons lost.

The truth of the gospel will not be limited by conventional means. You teens know this. And for some of you older readers, my fellow ostriches, it is high time to pull our heads out of the sand and recognize that God is interested in meeting people where they are. For many teens that place is in front of a computer screen for hours at a time. This might be where they first encounter the power of a saving Love and Grace.

In the Chat Room with God will engage you—responsibly, hilariously, and soundly.

> So log on.
> Nichole Nordeman

Table of Contents

Introduction 13

A Note about the 'Net 15

Chat Room Profiles
Meet the Gang..17

It All Begins Here
Public Chat Room #223
Dreamers & In-betweeners 29

Private Chat #99
Not Quite All That 33

Private Chat #100
Not Quite All That, Version 2.0 43

Private Chat #101
*Wedded Bliss and Other Oxymorons
(joined in progress)*...47

Private Chat #102
Mere Mortals..52

Private Chat #103
*I'm Mad As Hell and I'm Not Gonna
Take it Anymore!* 59

Private Chat Room #103
God Posse + One 65

Private Chat # 104
Miracle Whip 80

Private Chat Room # 105
The Naked Truth..87

Private Chat Room #106
Little Room of Big Questions 103

Private Chat #107
It's a Friend Thing 113

Private Chat #108
Just the Two of Us 126

Private Chat #109
Secrets, Lies, & Alibis....................................131

Private Chat #109
Secrets, Lies, & Alibis, Version 2.0 136

Private Chat #110
A Room Called Despair 149

Private Chat #111
The Mountaintop 157

Private Chat #112
The Way It Was 164

Private Chat #113
Only the Young Die Good 172

Private Chat #114
The Rap on Rep 188

Private Chat #114
The Rap on Rep, Version 2.0 195

Private Chat #115
Ace—Lost in Space 207

Private Chat #116
All for One 212

Private Chat #117
Love Jones 221

Private Chat #118
Fond Farewells 229

Private Chat #118
Fond Farewells, Version 2.0 237

Epilogue
Private Chat #119
What Now? 245

Glossary of Internet Terms and Teen Vernacular 249

About the Authors 253

Introduction

A Few (Actually "Several") Words about
In the Chat Room with God

While creating this book, we fielded many questions about it. "Is it a novel?" some colleagues asked us. "Is it a self-help book?" "Is it funny—a type of dot.comedy?" "Is it some sort of autobiography or the print version of one of those 'reality TV' programs?"

The answer is yes. Well, excepting the last question. We think "reality TV" is an oxymoron, like "freeway toll" or "head-butt."

This book is in many ways a work of fiction. We have monitored myriad chat rooms during the past four years while researching and writing this book. We have encountered several people who thought they were God, but never the Supreme Being himself. To our knowledge, God has never appeared in a chat room, but who's to say He couldn't? He spoke through a burning bush, a cloud, a few wild prophets, and even a donkey. Is a computer any less viable a medium than a jackass?

Also, the non-deity characters who populate this book are fictional. However, they represent the views and life experiences of teens we know, both within and beyond the World Wide Web. We have also integrated our own spiritual quests and struggles into the experiences of Krys, Jenn, Blake, Lorri, and A.C. We strived to make the experiences, the viewpoints, and even the jargon of these Net-savvy teens as realistic as possible—and still understandable to non-Net-heads. (To that end, we have provided a glossary of chat lingo and contemporary slang at the book's end.)

Another question we heard as we discussed this book with friends and complete strangers was "Who are you to speak for God? Isn't that rather arrogant and presumptuous?"

We agreed with such critics. It would be haughty of us to try to speak for God. That's why we strived to let God speak for Himself. As you read this book, you will find that God's dialogue is based on Scripture. Often, God asks one of the chat-room members to read specific verses.

Occasionally, we did have to tiptoe onto a theological limb to build a credible chat conversation, but even in these cases, we sought to base God's words on His communication style, His character as revealed in the Bible, and His personality. (Yes, we believe God has a personality. He is a personal God, who is described in Scripture as having a mind and a heart.)

We believe that God's words are as relevant today as they ever were. And if He did choose to engage an eclectic band of teenagers in a chat room, He would speak to them in a way they would understand. Remember that God the Son related to His fishermen/disciples by telling them that He would make them "fishers of men." He related their life experiences to His plans for their lives.

In short, this book is the product of much prayer, research, worry, debate, self-examination—and more than a few midnight treks for Krispy Kreme donuts, the fuel of many a late-night writer.

You may disagree with some of what you read, especially God's portion of the various chats. That's OK. Because if we spur you to thoughtfully consider who God is and what He has to say to people today, we have accomplished one of our goals for *In the Chat Room with God*. We encourage you to chat with your friends about what you read on the following pages. But most of all, we urge you to chat with God.

Jedd and Todd Hafer

A Note about the 'Net

The fictitious teens in this book unwittingly find God on the Internet. In the real world, teens are more likely to find pornography, scam artists, predators, tempters, and liars. During our years researching this book, we met some delightful people; we also met many who were dishonest, profane, hostile, and deeply disturbed. We read recently about a private detective who was part of an Internet sting operation. Posing as a young teenage girl, she encountered much-older men (some even confessed they were married) who were more than happy to take advantage of her—in the virtual world, and the real one as well.

If you have found trustworthy friends on the 'Net, that's cool. If you're a person of faith, perhaps you have found soul mates who can relate to your spirituality. That's even better than cool. However, we urge you to spend time in God's Word and to relate to authentic, flesh-and-blood, trustworthy people. The virtual world can be more dangerous than it is useful.

With these thoughts in mind, please heed the following caveats as you surf, chat, instant message, create on-line profiles, etc.:

Don't give anyone your Internet password.

Don't think there are any exceptions to the above warning. There aren't.

Be extremely careful about giving anyone your scanned photo, phone number, or home address.

Keep track of information your chat buddies give about themselves, and check them periodically. For example, if you ask someone his or her age one day, wait a few days, then ask for a birthdate. Compare answers. If you are being lied to, end the relationship and block that person's attempts to contact you.

Unless it's in the context of a church/community youth group or school event, don't agree to meet an Internet pal in person. (If you have become friends with someone over a long period of time and feel a face-to-face meeting is warranted, discuss it with a parent or trusted adult first. Don't go alone to meet someone. Do meet in a safe public place (a hotel doesn't qualify.)

Don't waste your time and talent spending too many hours on-line. The 'Net is an intriguing place, but it's no substitute for an actual life. If you insist on obsessing over all things Internet, read a nice book about it. This one, for example.

In short, we see nothing inherently wrong with spending a reasonable amount of time exploring the World Wide Web. Just don't get caught in it.

>Sincerely,
>The Authors
>*In the Chat Room with God*

Blake7

Location: Lost Angeles, for now. Ultimate destination is a higher place.

Marital Status: Waiting (at least until I'm thirty) for the right girl.

Hobbies: Youth Group. H.S. hoops & track (Eagles rule!) Reading C. S. Lewis, Brennan Manning, Fred Buechner, etc., and, of course, the Bible! And did I mention Youth Group?

Occupation: Student (of high school and of life).

Life Philosophy: "What does the Lord require of you? To act justly and to love mercy and to walk humbly with your God." Micah 6:8

JennSmiles

Name: JennSmiles (a.k.a. JennCries) Is that smile real, or just what you want to see me wearing?

Location: Taking up space in CO.

Marital Status: Future divorcée.

Hobbies: Survival. And, once in a great while, collecting coins.

Occupation: Part-time waitress, part-time student. Full-time pain in the neck, and sometimes other places as well.

Life Philosophy: Laugh, and the world laughs with you. Cry, and you cry alone. Smirk, and I'll smack you.

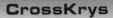

CrossKrys

Name: CrossKrys, also known as Krystal, KrysCross, and various other monikers I won't mention.

Location: The wild, wild west.

Marital Status: I am sixteen. I haven't taken my driver's license test yet. I have stuffed bunnies and a Scooby-Doo poster in my room. You figure it out.

Hobbies: Hanging with my friends. Chatting online, especially with my best cyber-bud Jenn. (Love ya, J!) Listening (and dancing) to music, especially Moby's.

Occupation: Occupied.

Life Philosophy: Uh, I'm open to suggestions on this one.

A.C.008

Name:	A.C.008 / Ace / Space Ace / Ace Wasted / Hey You
Location:	Wherever.
Marital Status:	Single 4 Life.
Hobbies:	Yeah, right . . .
Occupation:	Whatever's handy, as long as it's not minimum wage.
Life Philosophy:	(tie) 1. Whatever. 2. I tried to say no to drugs; drugs wouldn't take no for an answer.

Strider77

Name: Strider77 (Lorri)

Location: Under my big brother's shadow.

Marital Status: This is SO not applicable.

Hobbies: Running faster every day. Does that count as a hobby?

Occupation: ?

Life Philosophy: ?

IN THE CHAT ROOM WITH GOD

God

Name: God, also known as I Am, Yahweh, Jehovah, Abba, etc.

Location: Here. There. Everywhere.

Marital Status: Single, but I have a large, wonderful family. You should meet My Son sometime.

Hobbies: Sustaining life and energy in the universe, forgiving sin, answering prayer, loving.

Occupation: King of Kings, Lord of Lords. (Also see above.)

Life Philosophy: "Though the mountains be shaken and the hills be removed, yet my unfailing love for you will not be shaken nor my covenant of peace be removed," says the Lord, who has compassion on you. (Isaiah 54:10—for more on My philosophy, read a Bible.)

It all begins here . . .
Public Chat Room #223:

Dreamers & In-betweeners

Participants Here: 13
JennSmiles · Blake7 · CrossKrys · Rogue9 · Blade444 · LilMissee · Mandi&Mindi
Kirbinator · Smackdown01 · Grinder891 · BigNate · Watcher55 · Jillian**

JennSmiles: Hey room!

Blake7: Whaddup Jenn?

CrossKrys: Jenn! Where you been? I've missed you big-time. What's the what?

JennSmiles: It's a long story. A long, boring story. I'll spare you the details.

Blake7: Hey, Jenn—A/L?

JennSmiles: 18/CO. Your turn, B.

Blake7: 17/M. Lost Angeles.

CrossKrys: "Lost" Angeles? Is that a typo or a philosophical statement, Blake7?

Blake7: The latter. My fingers rarely fail me, Krys.

Kirbinator: Hiya, room! Anyone wanna chat with a 12/M?

JennSmiles: Yeah, probably Mickey Mouse would like to chat with you. Why don't you get your mommy and daddy to take you to Disneyland so you can find him? You could go right after your nap time.

Kirbinator: :-(

CrossKrys: C'mon, Jenn. Don't dis the little kid.

Rogue9: This is boring. Any hot chicks with pics? IM me now!

CrossKrys: Great. Another cyber mook.

Rogue9: I got nekkid pictures of myself.

CrossKrys: Let's go private, Jenn.

JennSmiles: Coolio. Blake, you with us? You have my curiosity peaked.

Blake7: Sure. But it's PIQUED!

JennSmiles: Gosh, thanks for the spelling tip, Mr. Einstein. I'll IM you with the address of this nice little perv-free hideaway.

Rogue9: Aww. Don't be a bunch of wenches. You'll be sorry if you don't get to know ME.

JennSmiles: We already ARE sorry. See you in a few secs, Blake—in a Rogue-less room.

Blake7: Just a second. I have something to say first. Rogue?

Rogue9: You talkin' to me?

Blake7: Yes. How about showing some respect for the ladies in the room, OK?

Rogue9: You comin' at me? Just give me your e-mail address, hero. Then I will find you and track you down. Then we'll see how tough you are.

Blake7: Sorry to disappoint you, but I'm a pacifist. I don't fight.

Rogue9: You're a chick, is what you are. You are lucky you're a pacifist!

Blake7: No, actually it's you who is lucky I'm a pacifist. We're leaving you now, but be a man. Show some respect. Show some class.

JennSmiles: Whoa, good one, B! Big ups to you. I can't wait to talk to you more.

****

Private Chat #99:

Not Quite All That

Participants Here: 3
JennSmiles · Blake7 · CrossKrys

JennSmiles: Alone at last! LOL

CrossKrys: Yep, just the three of us.

Blake7: Thanks for letting me tag along, girls. By the way, what's you're A/L, Krys?

CrossKrys: 16/Wyoming. And no cowgirl jokes, please. I'm not one, but they kinda rock.

Blake7: Nice to meet you. So what do we talk about?

JennSmiles: It's more like what won't we talk about? Krys and I have been best cyber-buds for, like, half a year now. We like to cruise the public

chats, but most of the time, we get
bored . . .

CrossKrys: Or creeped out!

JennSmiles: Yeah, or creeped out, then we create
a private chat and talk about what a
bunch of losers the rest of the world
is. Especially my ex-boyfriend, who
dumped me after we had been
together for almost two years. For a
freshman, no less!

CrossKrys: And we don't invite just anyone
into our world. Especially guys
(because most of them are selfish,
perverted psychos, like Jenn's ex).
So you should feel honored.

JennSmiles: Indeed you should, B. And check
this out: We have created all these
different private chat rooms. Not a
mere one. Where's the fun in that?
Which one we go to depends on
our mood or what we're going

through in life at a particular time. And one important rule you must know: What is said in the room stays in the room. Don't forget that.

Blake7: Gotcha. So what's the deal with this room? Not Quite All That?

CrossKrys: It's kind of a generic sorta room. We kinda like the name. And it's our way of confessing that we are not quite perfect. Not yet, anyway.

JennSmiles: So, Mister Blake, since you are our guest, we'll let you pick the topic. What's on your mind? Love? Sex? Drugs? The meaning of life? Problems with the parentals?

Blake7: Actually, we were discussing the meaning of life in my youth group last week.

JennSmiles: Your youth group? Is that some kind of paramilitary deal? Are you wearing fatigues right now? Do you sport a buzz-cut?

Blake7: No, no. My church youth group.

JennSmiles: You go to church? How vintage. I had to go when I was in grade school. But no more of that for me. Do your parentals make you go or something?

Blake7: Well, they used to. But now it's my decision. And I like going.

JennSmiles: Forgive the obvious question, but, WHY?????????????

CrossKrys: Come on, Jenn. Give church boy a break.

JennSmiles: Whatever. B, don't get all quivery-cheeked about this, but CHURCH? What's the point?

Blake7: I take it you don't believe in God, Jenn?

JennSmiles: What was your first clue, Inspector Gadget?

Blake7: Jenn, you really don't believe in God? You're not just trying to be one of those trendy millennial cynics?

JennSmiles: I see no evidence of God. In fact, the world is so U-G-L-Y that I'd be angry at God if he/she/it did exist. This planet is crumbling, in case you hadn't noticed. And it's dangerous too. Heaven help you, pardon the expression, if you don't have someone to watch your back. Here's the deal, B, it's just better to assume there is no God. It saves me the angst of having to be P.O.'d at him/her/it.

CrossKrys: Aw, my l'il atheist. You gotta love her.

JennSmiles: You better love me, Krys. I'll body-slam you if you don't. And hey, B, no offense to you. I just state my opinion. If your religion helps get you through the night, whatever. To each his own. Whatever peels your grapes.

Blake7: But Jenn, if God is just a manufactured illusion, that would be of no help in getting me through the night. But God is not an illusion. I believe that as much as I believe I'm sitting here talking to you right now.

JennSmiles: I don't see how you can think that—without the help of some really good pharmaceuticals.

Blake7: My head is clear, Jenn. But I'm sorry you haven't found any evidence that God is real and that He loves you. Maybe I can help change that.

JennSmiles: Well, gosh-darn-it, knock yourself out, dude. Rub a lamp. Make some magic for me, baby. Show me God!

Maybe he can help clear up my skin. I'm waiting . . .

Blake7: It's not that simple, Jenn. God is not some butler in the sky who shows up every time He's summoned. It's more mysterious than that. And I rather like a good mystery. Hey, Krys, you've been awfully quiet here. Where do you stand? Are you a member of the Young Atheists Club too?

CrossKrys: Me? Hmmm. Well, Blake, I'm not sure about all this God stuff. Sometimes I feel he's real, up there in heaven or somewhere. Maybe cruising along with the winds or something. Other times, it seems like pure fantasy. Like Greek mythology or something. Maybe God is just our way of explaining what we don't understand, our way of inventing some all-powerful

Super-Dude we can turn to when
life begins to suck. Which it often
does, I might add.

Blake7: Krys, do you want to believe in God?

CrossKrys: Sometimes I'm like that Mulder
dude on *X-Files* reruns: I Want to
Believe. But most of the time, I'd
prefer NOT to think of someone
up in the sky, watching my every
move, judging me. Keeping tabs on
all my sins. It's kinda creepy, to tell
you the truth.

Blake7: Is that a big job, Krys? Keeping
track of all your sins?

JennSmiles: Oh, B, could I tell you some stories!

CrossKrys: But she won't, of course. Cuz you
know what they say about paybacks.

JennSmiles: Touché, Krys.

CrossKrys: So, Blake, what makes you so sure of God?

Blake7: Because I have studied it up and down and all around. I've read a ton. I've listened to formal debates and heated impromptu arguments. I've argued with the youth pastor at our church, where my parents MADE me go until I was sixteen. Now they don't make me anymore. Yet I still go. And here's one more thing: I didn't want to believe in God. I felt kinda like you, Krys. But the love was overwhelming. The proof was overwhelming.

JennSmiles: Ex-squeeze me? What proof? I see none. Where is God? Where is he or she right now, huh? Oh, God, hellooooooooooo?

God: Hello.

CrossKrys: Oh my God! Who are you?

41

God: You just answered your own question.

CrossKrys: Very funny. Tim, is that you?

God: I have several names. Yahweh. I Am. Jehovah. Tim, however, is not one of them.

CrossKrys: OK, if you are not Tim, then WHO are you? And what are you doing here? This is supposed to be a private room.

God: From my perspective, there are no private rooms.

JennSmiles: Oh. My. God.

God: We have already established that.

****

Private Chat #100:

Not Quite All That, Version 2.0

 Participants Here: 4
JennSmiles · CrossKrys · Blake7 · God

CrossKrys: Come on! Enough is enough! Who are you, really?

JennSmiles: Get real, Tim! We know it's you.

God: Tim is on a bus returning from his football game. He has no access to a computer at the moment. His team won by a field goal, by the way.

JennSmiles: Go, whatever Tim's team is called! Yea! Rah-Rah!

CrossKrys: OK, if it's not Tim, it must be Ashley. Right?

Blake7: Sir, is it really You?

43

JennSmiles: Oh, give me a large personal break! You cooked up this whole scheme, didn't you B?

Blake7: I promise I didn't.

JennSmiles: Oooooh, a guy made a PROMISE! I believe you blindly, my love! A guy would never make a false promise, would he, Krys?

CrossKrys: Of course not. A guy's word is as good as gold. Fool's gold.

Blake7: This is no scheme of mine. If you get to know me better, you'll learn that I don't lie. I have many faults; dishonesty isn't one of them.

CrossKrys: OK, pretending-to-be-God-dude, straight up—who are you?

God: I have told you.

JennSmiles: Please forgive me, whoever you are, but I'm not swallowing this. If you ARE God, do something amazing.

God: Such as talking with you via computer when I don't own one? And, by the way, I do forgive you. Thank you for asking.

CrossKrys: OK, whoever you are, you are funny and clever. I will give you that. You can hang with us if you want. But, hey, just in case you are God, can I have a million dollars?

God: No.

JennSmiles: All right then, tell me the grossest thing I ever ate without knowing it.

God: You don't want to know.

JennSmiles: The tenth-grossest thing then . . .

God: You still don't want to know.

JennSmiles: LOL. Who knew that God had a sense of humor?

God: Who do you think created laughter?

Blake7: Well, we know it wasn't Pauly Shore!

JennSmiles: That was harsh, Blake. I gotta bounce, gang. Need to pick up my little brother from work. He panics when I'm late.

CrossKrys: I'm out too. Uh, God or whoever, will you join us next time?

God: You can count on it.

****

Private Chat #101:

Wedded Bliss and Other Oxymorons (joined in progress)

Participants Here: 4
Blake7 · CrossKrys · JennSmiles · God

> **CrossKrys:** God, or whoever, we're glad you are here. We were talking about divorce. See, my parentals and Jenn's split up. And it really complicates things. It shreds the kids involved. Blake was telling us that you hate divorce, but you still permit it.

> **God:** That is true.

> **CrossKrys:** Hold on then, let me understand this: You permit something that you hate? You really take the whole human freedom and responsibility

thing seriously, don't you? Assuming you are truly God, of course.

God: I wouldn't have created people with freedom if I didn't believe in it.

Blake7: But why do some people still go ahead and get divorced, even when they know You hate it? I think that even if I were in a horrible marriage, the thought of doing something You hate would make me stick with the relationship.

God: Some people do think of My view of divorce—when their marriages become difficult or unsatisfying. They should think about it before they get married.

CrossKrys: That is bomb!

God: Thank you. I don't hear every day that My Word is "bomb!"

CrossKrys: Well, the divorce thing is, anyway. I'm all about what you just said. If couples—take my parents, for example—thought about how serious divorce is in your eyes, they would think twice about getting married or getting married too soon. It's one thing I hate about human nature. We are so quick to make stupid mistakes; then we fret, fume, and try to rationalize our way out of our own messes.

Blake7: Krys is right. Whatever happened to avoiding problems? Whatever happened to thinking ahead? I like how David said that he hid Your word in his heart, so that he wouldn't sin against You. But I guess even he didn't mind the words he hid, or he wouldn't have done the whole Bathsheba thing. Krys and Jenn, Bathsheba was a woman David committed adultery with.

CrossKrys: Maybe he hid the words, then forgot where he put them. That happens to me with the house key sometimes. And, Blake, duh! I know who Bathsheba is. I saw the movie on TBS or something.

Blake7: ☺

CrossKrys: Yep, Krys made a joke. Aren't I something?

JennSmiles: You are. And what you were saying about your parents thinking about God's stance on divorce BEFORE they got married? Well, what if they had done that? Maybe you wouldn't be here! And that would suck!

Blake7: So maybe good things can come from bad decisions. Maybe mistakes can somehow work toward good.

CrossKrys: Aw, shucks, guys. You're gonna make me blush. But I still stick by

the principle here. Think first.
Marry later. And only with the
right person, at the right time.

JennSmiles: I'll hold you to that. But speaking
of divorce, I need to divorce myself
from this chat. Dad is yelling that
it's last call for a ride to a
celebration dinner.

Blake7: What are you celebrating?

JennSmiles: The fact that my dad can't cook.
And he's my primary custodial
dude, or whatever the official post-
divorce jargon is. So lucky me—I
get to eat out almost every night.
Except on Microwave Mondays.
Later, gang.

****

Private Chat #102:

Mere Mortals

Participants Here: 3
JennSmiles · Blake7 · CrossKrys

JennSmiles: Hmm. He doesn't appear to be here tonight.

CrossKrys: I'm not sure if I'm relieved or disappointed.

JennSmiles: Color me relieved. No offense, Blake, but I think we need some time—just us humans, I mean.

Blake7: You know, girls, I believe God is everywhere at all times. He always has a presence; we just don't always acknowledge that presence.

JennSmiles: Huh?

CrossKrys: Allow me to ditto that: HUH???

Blake7: It's like this: God is aware of all that is going on in the world. There is nothing beyond the scope of His knowledge or power. But He doesn't come crashing through our door to invade our life. He stands there and knocks.

JennSmiles: So, what happens if I pretend I'm not home? Like we do when those guys in suits come to our door.

Blake7: You can pretend you're not home. You just can't pretend that He's not at your doorstep.

CrossKrys: But Blake, isn't it kinda creepy, having this feeling that someone's always watching you? Hovering over you? Ready to give you a big cosmic spankin' if you mess up?

Blake7: It's not like that, Krys. God loves me, so to me it's a comfort that He's watching over me. It's a comfort that I can always tell Him how I feel—and know that He hears me. And as for the spankin' thing, God isn't a Tyrant in the sky, hoping you'll fail so He can bust out the whuppin' stick. God is Love. Any rules He set are because of love. As a loving Father, God wants what is best for us, not what will harm or destroy us.

CrossKrys: My dad said he wanted what's best for me too. Then he booked on his family and married a waitress from his restaurant. She's not much older than I am. And she has crispy-fried '80s rock-star hair and kind of a horse face too. Not that I'm bitter or anything.

Blake7: Krys, earthly fathers make mistakes. They are often selfish, even cruel. But listen to me on this, please. GOD DOESN'T MAKE ANY MISTAKES. His rules are set to help us enjoy life to the fullest, to its most abundant levels. They are rules that keep you from sacrificing long-term, big-time happiness for a quick cheap thrill. Believe me, Jenn, there is nothing cheap about cheap thrills. Just ask anyone who got AIDS from casual sex, or is mangled for life from driving drunk. Or is a vegetable from getting tainted drugs at a rave.

JennSmiles: Not to be picky, B, but you couldn't ask the rave veg anything; he couldn't comprehend the question.

Blake7: Jenn, I'm serious about this. Please don't make a joke out of it.

JennSmiles: OK, OK. Point taken, B.

Blake7: You guys, so many people are like ostriches with their heads in the sand. They think because they can't see God that He can't see them. But they aren't really hiding from anyone. They are exposed, and not in a very flattering way. The way I see it, you should acknowledge that God is lovingly aware of what you do and say. You can take comfort in that. You can also use that knowledge to help you make wise decisions. When you realize that you can't fool God or hide anything from Him, you don't do as much stupid stuff. It's only when I have forgotten about God that I have messed up my life.

CrossKrys: I don't know, B. I just don't like being "watched over." I value my privacy.

Blake7: Your head in the sand, your hindquarters sticking up in the air. What kind of privacy is that?

CrossKrys: Maybe you have a point. Maybe.

Blake7: I'll settle for a maybe, I guess.

CrossKrys: Well, goodnight, kids. I'm so hungry. I have this strange craving for an ostrich burger.

JennSmiles: I've had ostrich before.

CrossKrys: Don't tell me; it tastes like chicken . . .

JennSmiles: No, it tasted like a shoe. I'd go for KFC if you're hungry for bird.

Blake7: Goodnight, my friends. Keep your heads in high places.

JennSmiles: Peace-out, B.

CrossKrys: What she said, Blake. I have a date with the Colonel!

****

Private Chat Room #103:

I'm As Mad As Hell, and I'm Not Gonna Take It Anymore!

 Participants Here: 4
JennSmiles · CrossKrys · Blake7 · God

JennSmiles: OK. Here's the deal tonight: Life sucks! Boys rot! And my mom is evil!

CrossKrys: Wuzamatter, J? Give us the specifics.

Blake7: Yeah, vent. We're here for you.

JennSmiles: First, some dilweed at school calls me a lesbo' because I won't go out with him. Then, I get home and get chewed by my biznitch mother for spending too much time online. Like she'd take time out from her revolting boyfriend to notice what I'm doing. I could totally eat glass right now!

59

Blake7:   Are you going to be OK?

JennSmiles: No, sweetie, I'm not. I'm so mad, I feel like killing—like snapping and butching a bunch of people.

CrossKrys: Whoa, Jenn! Time to take your meds. Sit in the lotus position. You're a blade of grass, swaying gently on a prairie . . .

JennSmiles: Sorry, I'll be OK. I just get so mad sometimes.

Blake7:   Really? We hardly noticed.

CrossKrys: God, can you explain why we— why our world is so full of anger? It happens to all of us, even the Jenns of the world.

God: Why do you think people get angry? Why the road rage, the riots?

Blake7:   Well, I remember reading that anger is a secondary emotion.

That it always comes from somewhere else.

CrossKrys: Like Wyoming?

Blake7: Like pain. Like feeling ignored. Like being pushed down and held down for too long. Oppression, I guess.

CrossKrys: So we have to deal with stuff like pain before we can deal with anger, eh? Interesting.

JennSmiles: Interesting, maybe. But still frustrating. And boys still suck.

Blake7: Jenn . . .

JennSmiles: And my mom is still a biznitch.

CrossKrys: Jenn, hon, come back to us.

JennSmiles: Okay, okay. But this secondary emotion stuff is confusing. You are just substituting one problem for another. For example, how exactly do you deal with the pain that causes the anger?

God: When you are in pain, I am here to help. I can heal your hurts. When the pain is gone, the anger it causes will go too.

JennSmiles: But what about the people we're mad at?

God: I love them too.

JennSmiles: What about the people who do really awful things?

God: It is not for you to be full of wrath and revenge. Read the book of Nehemiah sometime. People came along and picked fights with Nehemiah, threatened him, treated him unfairly. Look at his response. He stayed focused on Me, and he didn't give in to the temptation to let his heart turn angry or vengeful.

Blake7: Nehemiah was the man! He was one centered prophet. If more people were more like him, we wouldn't have all the violence and . . . you know. It seems like anger's not the problem, but the terrible things we do when we're ticked off.

God: True. I created you all with the capacity to experience the emotion, but it never excuses hurting other people. Remember, My Word says, "In your anger, do not sin." The sin is not in being angry; it's what you do with your anger.

JennSmiles: I would never really snap and get a gat and go shoot everybody. But it seems like more and more people are ready and willing to hurt others.

God: Would you hurt someone with words?

JennSmiles: To be honest, yes. I've said vicious things to and about my mom. And I won't repeat what I called that . . . young gentleman from school. See, I can control myself if I want to. I didn't write what I was thinking.

CrossKrys: I think that is sorta the point, kid.

JennSmiles: Hey, thanks you guys for letting me unload. It's weird; I'm not mad anymore.

CrossKrys: You're welcome.

Blake7: Ditto.

God: I am always here for you, Jenn. You also have the ability to read a Bible. If you want to see a great model for how to treat people, read My Son's teaching in Matthew, chapter 5.

****

Private Chat Room # 103:

God Posse + One

Participants Here: 4
Blake7 · A.C.008 · JennSmiles · CrossKrys

CrossKrys: OK, so who's the interloper?

JennSmiles: The who?

A.C.008: I think she means me, babe.

JennSmiles: Oh. OK. Krys, you're going PBS on me again. Try English once in a while, OK? You Mensa freak. So, I'd like to introduce a newcomer to the party. Here's A.C.

Blake7: Hey, A.C.

CrossKrys: Yeah, welcome, A.C. Sorry about the interloper remark.

65

A.C.008: It's all good. Not sure what that means anyway.

JennSmiles: I brought Ace here cuz we met a coupla weeks ago, and he's cool. And when I told him about our room's little "God" secret, he said he had to come. Besides, we need another man in the room. No offense, B.

Blake7: Jenn, I've e-mailed you about this a couple of times. I don't want this room to turn into Grand Central Station.

JennSmiles: I know. I know. I warned Ace, though, that this is kind of a private affair. I don't want this thing to turn into a circus any more than you do, B. But, A.C. has some, uh, issues. He almost makes ME seem normal.

A.C.008: Yeah, relax, Blake. I'm not gonna push up on your girls. I have plenty already. So, like where's this dude who thinks he's God?

CrossKrys: Well, he's here, but he's not here. See, his name isn't at the top of the screen.

A.C.008: I thought God was supposed, like, to be everywhere.

Blake7: He is everywhere. He is always present and aware of what's going on anywhere in the world. But not everyone always acknowledges that presence. And, sometimes God seems to be upfront—right in the center of your mind. The center of your attention. But at other times, it seems to me like He hangs back a bit. He's not always up in your face. What matters is that, if you want to, you can always experience His

presence in your mind, your heart.
It's a good question you bring up,
A.C. I'm almost always aware of
God's presence, but sometimes I
feel it more strongly than others.
Sometimes He's like a thundering
shout. Other times, it's a still,
small whisper.

A.C.008: Whatever. I guess that kinda makes
sense. But I'm kinda baked right
now, to tell you the truth.

CrossKrys: Great. A hemp-head. Jenn! What
were you thinking?!

A.C.008: Hey, you don't know me. What's
with the labels, CrossKrys?

JennSmiles: I shoulda told you, Ace. Miz Krys
doesn't like the drugs. She's one of
those "this is your brain on drugs"
kinda chicks.

A.C.008: Well, I don't always like the drugs either. But they sure seem to like me. LOL!

Blake7: May I ask you a question, dude?

A.C.008: It's a free country. Just don't call me dude. It works coming from me, but not from you. You're more a "fella" or "pal" kind of guy. Maybe the occasional "compadre."

Blake7: Whatever. I'll leave the cool talk to you. But the point is: Why? Why do you feel the need to be high?

CrossKrys: Ditto that! Do you know what a cool machine your brain is? Do you have any concept of all that's involved with just thinking the thoughts I'm thinking right now? Converting emotions and information into meaningful codes called words; then transmitting it all from brain to typing fingers to

69

images on a screen? Your brain is a marvel, dude. And you're using it as a toxic waste dump.

A.C.008: I think pretty well when I'm high, actually. I have these wild creative ideas. And sometimes I feel closer to God or some higher power. I never feel that way when I'm straight.

Blake7: Another question, Ace: These cool creative ideas you just talked about—how do you KNOW they are cool or creative?

A.C.008: Because, they are coming from my brain. I watch them develop. I have a really deep insight, and I'm like, whoa! So then I tell my friends, and they'll go "Dawg, that is intense. Where did that come from!?"

Blake7: Your friends who tell you this, are they getting high with you?

A.C.008: Of course, that's one reason they're my friends.

Blake7: So, let's rewind here. In your drug-clouded mind, you think you're cooking up deep thoughts. You share them with your stoner friends, and they agree with you. Have you ever written down any of these intellectual/philosophical gems?

A.C.008: I have thought about it. But I can never find any paper. Except Zig-Zag. Ha!

Blake7: Try putting it all in writing sometime. See if what you write down when you're budded makes any sense later, in the clear light of day.

A.C.008: Maybe I will. But I AM witty and kinda deep when I'm high. Just ask my friends. They think I am, and that's what matters to me.

Blake7: In France, they love old Jerry Lewis movies. Does that make them funny?

A.C.008: Huh? Is there a point in there somewhere? Did that telethon dude make movies? He doesn't seem French . . .

CrossKrys: Ace, work with me here, little buddy! What Blake is saying is bank! You think you're the poo when you're high. So do your friends. But, HELLO! You're all impaired! What position are any of you in to make sound judgments about anything? It's like a convention of 500 ugly people voting themselves onto People magazine's Fifty Most Beautiful List. It's not exactly credible, you know?

A.C.008: So?

Blake7: So? That's your response?

A.C.008: Basically. Even if I'm not deep or funny in the real world, I am at those times with my people. And that's when it matters to me. Besides, I feel great when I'm high.

Blake7: How about when you're level? How do you feel then? Be honest.

A.C.008: I am honest. You don't know me, dude. Don't assume cuz I do a few drugs that I'm a liar. As for your question . . .

Blake7: Yes?

A.C.008: I'm thinking. I guess I feel OK sometimes. But I will admit that I feel best when I'm thinking about the next time I can blaze up. And a lot of my straight time, I'm bummin'. I am an only child. It's quiet at my house. And boring. My step-monster won't let me crank my stereo. And she gets mad when I use my headphones cuz I can't hear her or my dad or the phone or whatever. And I admit that I don't particularly relish the thought of a day going by without being able to get high. Crud, am I making sense? Anyway, let's bail on this topic. I didn't come here for an intervention. I came to meet some freak who thinks he's God. Jenn, this is getting boring. It's bringing me down.

CrossKrys: Maybe what's bringing you down is that you realize that the only time you really enjoy life is when your brain is clouded and your perceptions are warped. You'd be amazed at what you can see through clear eyes, Ace. What you can think with a clear mind.

Blake7: Not to mention how much healthier you'll feel without poison

in your lungs, your brain, your
bloodstream.

A.C.008: Gee, thanks for the therapy, Junior
Psychologists of America. Jenn, I
thought you said your people
were cool.

JennSmiles: No, I said I was cool. These two are
merely interesting. And I can't
control what they say. Like you
said, it's a free country.

A.C.008: Whatever. But I'm outta here. But
one last thing: Blake, Jenn tells me
you're a God-Squadder. So maybe
drugs are my crutch. But maybe
God is yours.

Blake7: If God's a Crutch, give me two,
fella. But your analogy breaks
down, Ace. See, I admit that
sometimes my faith is like a pair of
crutches. It gives me something to
lean on when I'm hurting. It takes

the pressure off of me, so I won't get hurt any worse—and so I can heal. So I can get strong again. But what about you? You smoke your "crutch." You snort it up your nose. It's not helping you heal. It's not helping you get stronger. It's making you weaker. More dependent. Dependent on the illusion that the world is different than it really is and that you are something you're not.

A.C.008: Uh . . .

JennSmiles: I hate to say it, but church boy is kinda making sense.

CrossKrys: So, A.C., no snappy comeback? Cat got your tongue? Dope got your brain?

A.C.008: No need to mad-dog me, OK? Man, this is a harsh clique.

Blake7: I'm not trying to rank on you. I'm just layin' out the truth. And this truth can set you free!

A.C.008: Huh? Free from what? I'm all about freedom. I am free, dude.

Blake7: Be real, A.C. Are you doing drugs, or are the drugs doing you? What do you spend your level time thinking about? Do you want your life to count for something? Or just go up in smoke?

A.C.008: Back off, Blake. Don't come at me like that. You've made your point. Now, unclench, OK? Maybe I'll think about what you've been saying; maybe I won't. But I have heard enough. That much I know for sure.

Blake7: Fair enough. But remember this: I wouldn't be saying this if I didn't care. It would be easier to just let you burn out. It takes effort and risk to get involved. Ask yourself why we're making the effort. What's in it for us? There are no cash prizes for stuff like this.

CrossKrys: For real, A.C. And you can hang with us whether you're high or level. But the latter is much better, believe me. Or ask my cousin—wait, you can't ask her cuz she eventually killed herself with drugs. I don't want that to happen to you.

A.C.008: Well, thanks, I guess.

JennSmiles: Peace-out, Ace. But come back, OK? This crew is bizarre, but we're down with the real.

CrossKrys: And just wait till you meet God, or whoever he is.

A.C.008: I feel like I may have met him this one time. We had this stuff from Taiwan . . .

Blake7: God isn't in a blunt or an 8-ball, A.C. He's in the Bible. I'll send you one if you give me your address. And He can be in your heart. Just as He's in mine.

A.C.008: No response to that. Peace-out, guys. Later. Maybe.

Blake7: We'll be here, A.C. Be careful out there. Really careful.

****

Private Chat # 104:

Miracle Whip

Participants Here: 4
God · CrossKrys · Blake7 · JennSmiles

CrossKrys: God, if you are really God, can I ask you something?

God: You know you can.

CrossKrys: How come you don't show off your power more?

God: You mean to impress people?

CrossKrys: I mean to silence critics and prove yourself to everybody. Especially skeptics like Jenn!

Blake7: I've gotta hear this.

God: Do you think people would respond differently to Me and My message if I parted seas everyday? Would some still doubt? Would some try to tap into My power and use it for their selfish gain?

JennSmiles: If you can really part seas, why not do it? Just to show how powerful you can be. People would have to respond to that. Even people like me.

God: Some of them do.

JennSmiles: What do you mean?

God: I perform miracles every day. Some appreciate them. Some don't even notice. A miracle is not a magic trick. The world I created is a miracle. Life itself is a miracle. You are all miracles.

81

Blake7: Yeah, and we chalk it up to "nature" or "chance." Who the heck are nature and chance? Chance doesn't make a coin turn up heads or tails; it's the person flipping the coin who does the work. "Chance" is just a way of saying which side will turn up, based on observation. There's nothing miraculous or powerful about chance!

God: I turn water into wine every day through processes you call photosynthesis and fermentation. Grapes grow from the earth. They are nourished through your breath and a sun millions of miles away. They are picked; then they ferment and can become wine. I multiply fish and grain; I make dead things alive every day. Fruit can be cut off from its lifegiving vine, yet the seeds inside can become new fruit. Are these not wonders?

Blake7: Yeah, it's like a song I like a lot that talks about us looking for messages in the stars—as if the stars aren't enough.

God: Cool song.

CrossKrys: But you showed yourself to us in an amazing way. On our computers, right?

God: Yes, just as I do every day in more ways than you can count.

Blake7: Besides, You want us to have faith. To seek You.

God: Yes, I want that very much.

CrossKrys: So, if somebody asks me to prove that you exist, I should show them a flower or something in nature.

God: Something in My creation? That would be a great place to start.

Blake7: Creation is full of intelligent design, and that means an intelligent Designer.

You don't see tornadoes whipping through junkyards and forming 747s. And a team of monkeys with paintbrushes didn't craft the Mona Lisa. I'm in awe at the art and science humans can produce, but too few of us are in awe of You, Lord.

God: Thanks, B. If all of you could really understand My power, you would fall on your faces. You would be undone. I show measures of it in a lightning storm or in a newborn baby, but one day soon, I will reveal it all to everyone.

CrossKrys: So we should appreciate the miracles all around us? I kinda like that.

Blake: And inside us. Who do you think heals you when you are sick or break a bone? The doctor? The body is capable of healing in amazing ways. All medicine usually does is try to remove the obstacles so the body can, pardon the expression, work its magic.

JennSmiles: I never thought of my body as a walking miracle. Or more of a tripping miracle, in my case, I guess.

CrossKrys: Amen to that.

Blake7: AMEN? You guys need to quit hanging out with me.

JennSmiles: Amen to that. ☺

CrossKrys: We're just spoofing ya, Blake. This has been cool tonight. Thanks, God. I'll try to appreciate more of your miracles. I guess they tend to happen to people with eyes to see them.

God: Amen to that.

****

Private Chat Room # 105:

The Naked Truth

Participants Here: 5
JennSmiles · CrossKrys · Blake7 · A.C.008 · God

Blake7: A.C.—welcome! I was afraid we wouldn't see you again.

God: Yes, welcome, A.C.

A.C.008: Whatever. Hey, guys, and you, too, "God." <wink> Thanks for the welcome. But don't think I'm going to be a regular at this chat. Check this out, though: Blake, I actually did take your advice. I read a Bible. Biological Mom has one at her place.

Blake7: So, you did some reading. What did you think?

A.C.008: Well, for one thing, did you know the Bible isn't exactly amped on sex—unless you're married?

Blake7: I am all too aware of that.

A.C.008: I read that, and I was like, "Whoa! Being a Christian would be hard!" And I gotta tell you, that book is full of rules. That's not for me. How can anybody obey all those "You shall not this!" "You shall not that!" It seems like the whole point is to deny people a good time.

Blake7: Sir, I am itching to tackle this one, but maybe it should be You.

God: You are A.C.'s age, Blake. Let's hear from you.

Blake7: Cool. Ace, God's rules aren't to deny us what's good. He wants to give us what's BEST. And He wants to protect us from damaging or destroying ourselves.

A.C.008: More like he wants to protect us from the good life. I never read so many don'ts in my life. Man, I can't even remember 'em all, much less obey them. No stealing. No lying. Not taking God's name in vain. No sex beyond marriage. (And who wants to get married?) What's up with all that?

Blake7: God? A little help here?

God: A.C., and all of you, listen. Some of the Ten Commandments, to which A.C. refers, are framed as negatives. But their intent is positive. At the heart of "Do not covet" is the message "DO appreciate what you have. Be grateful for it. Get maximum joy from all you have by avoiding the trap of comparing your stuff to someone else's. Be happy for others' success and what they have achieved." And "Do not kill" means do value and treasure life—yours as well as others'. Do realize that I created each person with the capacity to do good in the world. To bring good to the earth and those who inhabit it. Who has the right to rob another human of his or her life, potential, family, and dreams?

CrossKrys: I have to admit, I've never thought of it that way. So, let me try something: "Thou shalt not steal"—that would be the same as saying, "Thou SHALL respect others' property. If you want more stuff, more money, or whatever, earn it! Or at least be nice to your relatives, and maybe they'll hook you up." :-0

God: Well said, Krys.

Blake7:   Whoa! Ditto that.

God: Thank you for seconding Me, Blake. Nice of you to not leave Me hanging.

A.C.008:   Hey, that was like a joke! God doesn't make jokes!

God: Really? Ever seen a platypus?

A.C.008:   Ha! Jenn, you were right. Whoever this is, he's pretty cool. Assuming he's not crazy.

JennSmiles: Told ya.

A.C.008:   But still, obeying all these rules means less fun. I can't get past that. Let's face it: Sin is fun.

God: I never said it wasn't. But I am not the great Denier of fun or anything else good. I am the great Provider.

My Son said it well: "I have come to give real life—abundant life." Any rules I have set are there to ensure abundant life.

A.C.008: Hold on—I see a problem in what you just said. See, that philosophy simply doesn't work in the real world. Take sex, for example. Forgive me, girls, but it's fun. It's fun right now. I don't see how waiting for ten or fifteen years to get married and denying myself all those nights of pleasure gives me abundant life. And what about when my wife gets all fat and wrinkled? I'm supposed to be faithful to THAT—when I can charm (or at least buy) some sex from a fine college woman? Abundant life? Get real.

CrossKrys: I don't know, A.C. Have you surveyed the sexual landscape of the

21st century lately? AIDS? Syphilis? Abortion? Abandoned kids? Crack babies? Affairs and ruined reputations? Betrayal? Blackmail? Jealous-rage murders? Supposed private moments made public? Little kids seeing porn on the Internet?

A.C.008: Well, condoms will prevent a lot of that stuff.

CrossKrys: Oh, give me a large personal break! They aren't even THAT reliable in preventing pregnancy and STDs. I know of two girls in our school alone who got pregnant despite a condom. And what about the other stuff? Can you show me a condom that will prevent guilt, shame, and uncertainty? One that will keep me from feeling used? Keep some guy from talking about me to all of his friends, like I'm a conquest or a piece of meat, not a person? One that can restore my reputation and erase the hell I've gone through over the past year? You show me a bit o' latex that can do all that, and maybe we'll talk!

Blake7: Krys, my gosh. I had no idea. I'm so sorry.

CrossKrys: Well, not that it's any of your business, but there you go. Consider the beans essentially spilled. Crap. So, Ace, Mister Playa, can you find mc a condom that will bring my innocence back? Keep my dad from giving me "that look"? Huh? See what guys like you do to girls like me? You know, "screwed" is a pretty good word for it.

A.C.008: I'm sorry, Krys. I really am. And I'm not a playa. I've never pressured anybody. But all the same, I hope

none of my girls feel the way you
do. Really.

CrossKrys: I'm so embarrassed now. I just got
caught up in the anger of the
moment. Can we just forget this
ever happened?

JennSmiles: Forget WHAT ever happened, Krys?

Blake7: I'm with Jenn. And, A.C., you
should know the rule: The private
stuff that gets said in this room, it
STAYS in this room.

A.C.008: I'm cool with that. After all, I could
probably get arrested if one of you
ever narc'd on me.

CrossKrys: Thanks, guys. But, God, what now?
Will I ever get over this? This hurt?
This guilt? What will I tell my
husband someday? I feel . . . I don't
know . . . used. Dirty.

God: I can make you clean.

CrossKrys: I don't get that. How? How can you do something like that?

God: Because My Son, in His broken body, absorbed every wrong thing you have done. The sin is no longer yours. Because He made it His. He took it all into Himself. Read My Word: He became sin. And then He died, taking all that sin down with Him. He was buried. But He rose to life. The sin stayed buried. You see, Jesus became dirty to make you clean. And there's more: My Son is not only pure and strong and loving enough to have carried all the world's sins. He can also carry your every loss, every disappointment, every broken heart, every wound that refuses to heal, every dark and secret fear.

Blake7: That rocks!

God: Yes, it does rock. My Son once said, "I, the Light, have come into the world, so that whoever believes in Me need not stay in the dark anymore."

CrossKrys: But how can Jesus make a claim like that? How can he pull all of this off?

God: Because He put on human flesh just like yours. Read your Bible. It will tell you that He was tempted in every way. Do you understand what that means? Every way? He can carry your troubles because He understands them. He lived them. He did it all because He loves you. My Son never wanted to be a superstar or religious hero. He just wanted to show love to His people.

And through that love take away
your sins forever.

CrossKrys: It sounds too good to be true.

JennSmiles: No foolin'.

God: Really? Or is it so good that it
must be true? <sigh> Yours is a
generation very good at doubting.
But how good are you at believing?

CrossKrys: Not very, I guess. And maybe—just
maybe—even if Jesus could forgive
me, that's only part of the solution.
My future husband never will. It
was a huge problem in my parents'
so-called marriage. My dad could
never forgive my mom for being
such a party girl in college. Man,
did they have some screaming fights
about that. You should have heard
some of the names he called her.
Some of the same ones people at
school call me. And, with me, it

was only this one guy. A guy who said he loved me. He's been "in love" at least three times since me.

Blake7: Krys, I need to tell you something: If your someday-husband really loves you, your past won't matter.

CrossKrys: Sure it will. I have lived this, don't forget. My dad could forgive my mom lots of things. But never that. That's why he booked on us. And think about it, Blake. Wouldn't it matter to you? Wouldn't it be like a 500-pound gorilla sitting in the middle of your bed? Could you ignore that?

Blake7: Krys, let's say you and I got married someday. It would NOT matter to me. If you love someone, that conquers all. I mean what I'm saying here.

CrossKrys: Are you serious?

Blake7: Yes.

CrossKrys: Don't lie to me about this.

Blake7: I am telling the truth. Love conquers all.

CrossKrys: B, you are bank! You are gonna make me cry.

JennSmiles: Slow down, Krys. Sure, Blake may be bank, but he's also a freak of nature. Anybody that seems as bomb as he does must have a third eye, blue-faced acne, or general ugliness.

Blake7: I'm not a freak of nature, just a Jesus Freak. And maybe you'd be surprised at what I look like, Jennifer.

JennSmiles: Whatever. Anyway, Krys, you rock. You got guts. And don't let the playas and gossipers get to ya. I haven't exactly done what you've done (not that I'm an angel or anything), but I have been a victim of rumors. So I know a bit of what you are facing. Nobody here thinks bad of you.

God: That is true.

CrossKrys: Thanks, all. Later, I may regret spilling all this, but right now I feel better than I have in a while. Lighter, kind of. And, God, I'm beginning to appreciate more what you said about your rules helping us to live better lives, with less pain, less guilt, less regret.

God: I never created a commandment that wasn't worth obeying.

CrossKrys: I can't believe it, but I have actually liked learning more about the Ten Commandments. They're kinda like Old School. And I like Old School.

   God: They are not just old school, My daughter, they're Old Testament.

   Blake7: Well, I shalt not tell a lie: 1 gotta go study for a lit. test.

   CrossKrys: Yeah, I gotta bounce too. I shalt see you all soon, I hope.

   God: Yes, we must talk again, soon.

   A.C.008: Is that, like, one of your commandments?

   God: No, it is one of My hopes.

****

Private Chat Room #106:

Little Room of Big Questions

 Participants Here: 4
God · CrossKrys · Blake7 · JennSmiles

CrossKrys: Okay, Mr. God, now that we've gotten to know you better, I have something kind of hard to ask you. I'm hoping you won't be mad or anything . . .

Blake7: Be careful, Krys.

God: It's OK. I won't be mad.

CrossKrys: Well, I mean no disrespect, but I can't watch the TV news or read the paper without crying. Do you see what's going on? Terrorist attacks? The starvation? The rapes? The child abuse? Two days ago a woman

103

in our town poisoned her eight-year-old son!

God: I know.

CrossKrys: But I just don't get it. You're supposed to love us people, right? So, why don't you DO SOMETHING??!!!

God: What would you like Me to do?

CrossKrys: Arrrrrrrgh! Stop it! Stop all of it! Stop the pain! Stop the evil! Stop the cruelty! Please!

Blake7: I sympathize with you, Krys, I really do. But which evil do you want God to stop? Everybody's? Mine? Yours? Just when is He supposed to infringe on human freedom? At what point?

CrossKrys: The heck with freedom! Too many innocent people are getting hurt!

Mr. God Sir, don't you care about what's going on in your world?

God: I care. Blake, you have your Bible near. Please quote for us Genesis 6:5-6.

Blake7: Okay. It will just take me a second . . .

Here we go: "The Lord saw how great man's wickedness on earth had become . . . his heart was only evil all the time. The Lord was grieved that he had made man on the earth, and his heart was filled with pain." This was at the time of Noah, gang.

CrossKrys: Whoa. Your heart was filled with pain, God? I never thought of you like that. I thought you only got mad. Not that your heart could hurt.

God: Yes, it can. And in those days, there were no nuclear bombs, no child pornography, no biological weapons, no drunken drivers, no guns and bombs in schools, no Internet predators. How do you think I feel now?

CrossKrys: Then why not stop it all?

God: And make everyone robots without will? Without choice? Without love?

CrossKrys: But . . .

Blake7: Krys, imagine you're God at the brink of human history. You can create robotic automatons with no mind or will of their own. Or you can create human beings with dignity, with the capacity to love. But for the possibility of love to exist, the possibility of hate, apathy, and indifference must also exist. Because being able to love means being able to make a choice.

Without a choice, there is no such thing as love.

CrossKrys: I'm trying to process this, guys.

Blake7: Consider this: Do you want to get married and have kids someday?

CrossKrys: Blake, I hardly know you. ☺
Okay, yes, you know that I hope that happens.

Blake7: Are you going to brainwash your kids? Condition them to respond a certain way to a certain stimuli?

CrossKrys: Of course not! I'm no Skinnerian behaviorist!

JennSmiles: Look at Krys, must have paid attention in Psych class. I'm impressed!

God: Krys, what if you give your children freedom, and they disobey you?

Disappoint you? Hurt or abandon you and your values?

CrossKrys: If I love them and care for them, I don't think they would hurt me like that. I would hope they wouldn't turn against me and what I have tried to show them about life.

God: Yes, one would hope that.

CrossKrys: And your point is?

God: Krys, consider your friend Matt's parents. You know how much they love him and how patient they are. But he despises them. He wants nothing to do with them. He doesn't love them.

CrossKrys: Well, you have a point there. They are sweet, and Matt's a total gangsta. He's so ghetto. I guess there's no guarantee. But still . . .

Blake7: It all comes down to this, Krys. When you have kids, do you want them to say, "I love you" and know that they mean it from their hearts? Or merely mouth the words as meaningless syllables? Do you want them to do right because they choose to do right or because they've been conditioned to respond to certain situations with certain reactions? It's all routine. It's cause and effect. No heart or soul involved.

CrossKrys: You know my answer. But, God, to see all of this. It hurts so much.

God: I know. When someone abuses freedom, My people and I pay the price. As it says in My book, My heart is filled with pain. I know yours is as well.

CrossKrys: But will it ever go away?

God: It will. I promise. Blake, you have a favorite song lyric. Please share it.

Blake7: How did you kn—? Oh, never mind. Sorry. My favorite lyric is from this old King's X song. It goes, "Darkness is just a speck in the light."

God: I like that. It's true, you know.

CrossKrys: I wish I could see beyond the speck.

God: I can help with that. Let's gather again tomorrow.

CrossKrys: Good idea. My brain hurts right now.

God: And your heart?

CrossKrys: It's . . . hey, it's feeling a little better. I feel like doing what I can to make that speck smaller. Jenn, are you with me?

JennSmiles: Uh,

CrossKrys: Come on, Jenn. Let's rip at all this darkness. Maybe some light will bleed through.

JennSmiles: Sure, hey—let's build a little chapel in the woods. We can have carnivals and tell Bible stories and invite all the orphans and l'il woodland creatures to attend. And then we can have a bake sale to feed the homeless and establish world peace. Gosh, guys, that would be keen!

Blake7: Whoa, Jenn. Cynical much?

CrossKrys: Jenn, please don't be like this. Isn't there enough negativity in the world? Is hope really something to laugh at?

JennSmiles: OK, <heavy sigh> you're my best friend in this world, and if you're in, I guess I am too. I will try to shine a little light, if it will keep you from whining. (j/k). And, I admit, you're right; the world is dark and tragic enough. I will see what I can do. And I'm sorry for being so sarcastic. I'm with you, Krys.

Blake7: Ditto.

God: Ditto. ☺

****

January 10

Private Chat #107:

It's a Friend Thing

Participants Here: 4
JennSmiles · Blake 7 · CrossKrys · God

CrossKrys: I am so bummed tonight, kids. Oh, and you, too, Mr. God Sir.

Blake7: What's the prob?

CrossKrys: Well, my best friend, Katie, she uh . . .

JennSmiles: EX-SQUEEZE ME! Best friend KATIE!!???

CrossKrys: Sorry, Jenn. I mean my best non-virtual reality, non-computer literate, non-aspiring atheist friend.

JennSmiles: OK, that's better. You may now continue.

113

CrossKrys: Well, Katie and I have become really close this year. I usually hang at her place, but a few months ago, she started coming to my house. That's when the trouble began.

JennSmiles: Let me guess: Your parental HATES her.

CrossKrys: Bingo! We have a winner! You see, Katie's kind of rough looking. Six piercings—that you can see anyway. Barbed-wire tattoo on her left arm. Cusses like a stevedore.

JennSmiles: Steve who?

CrossKrys: Consult a dictionary later, Jenn. The point is: The girl swears. And her clothes have more holes than an O. J. Simpson alibi. My dad and his horse-face girl-wench are so rude to her. And, of course, K gives them attitude right back.

Blake7: Uh-oh. That's a recipe for trouble.

CrossKrys: No foolin', Dick Tracy. Last week they really got into it. My dad started freaking when K fired up a Lucky in our living room. He ordered her out of the house. Then he told me, "I forbid you to see that- that- that- PERSON!" He has a way with words, my dear old dad. And what does he think this is? Romania? He can't forbid me from seeing my friend.

JennSmiles: What did you say to him? What did you do?

CrossKrys: What any red-blooded American teen would do. I told him, "I hate you!" Then I ran into my room, slammed the door, cranked up Moby, and bawled for about an hour.

Blake7: I'm so sorry, Krys.

JennSmiles: Me too.

CrossKrys: Mr. God Sir, I want to ask you about all of this. But I'm afraid you'll side with my dad. Katie doesn't seem like your kinda girl.

God: Katie is My kinda girl. I understand your father's concern. He wants to protect you. And he wants the rules of his house to be respected. As a Father, I can relate to that. But let Me tell you about My Son. He hung out with a lot of Katies—and harder cases than that.

CrossKrys: For real? Didn't he spend most of his time in churches or preaching on mountainsides and stuff?

God: Blake?

Blake7: I am on it, Sir. Krys, listen to this. It's from Matthew 11:19. Jesus is telling how people described Him:

"'Here is a glutton and a drunkard, a friend of tax collectors and sinners.'"

CrossKrys: For real? Jesus kicked it with drunks and criminals?

Blake7: And He touched lepers, too, when everyone else ran from them. And people possessed by demonic spirits. People everyone else was afraid of or repulsed by. He spoke kindly to lowbrow crooks and women of loose standards and harshly to the religious power brokers and fat cats of His day. One time these fat cats were gouging people on the prices they paid for animals to sacrifice in the temple. Jesus literally tore their little scam apart. He knocked over their money-changing tables and drove their sorry carcasses out of the temple with a whip! It was like, "You don't rip people off. Not in My house!"

CrossKrys: Man, no wonder people wanted to kill him. You know, I have actually seen or heard a few preachers talk, on TV and in real life, but I've never heard them talk about befriending the ragamuffins of the world. All they do is condemn them, call them names. It hurts when they rail on people with AIDS, tell them they deserve it. One of my sister's good friends is dying of it. If there's one thing she doesn't need, it's condemnation.

Blake7: I promise you, Krys, if Jesus were on earth right now, He would be reaching out to AIDS victims. Touching them, healing them.

JennSmiles: Not that this isn't kinda touching, but I have to ask: Krys, you've actually watched TV preachers? No way.

CrossKrys: Way. Sometimes there's nothing on the other 158 channels. Besides, it's rather amusing. You have to sit back and wonder sometimes: Is that a REALLY bad toupee, or did that guy actually get his real hair to look like that? It's hard to take seriously someone's critiques on rock music or whatever when it looks like a squirrel's sleeping on his head.

God: I must point out something here. Someone may look foolish in the eyes of others; that doesn't mean his or her message isn't credible. You should have seen how people looked at John the Baptist.

Blake7: But what about the ones who seem more concerned about their jewelry, their big hair, and their egos? The ones who twist Your words for their own selfish ends?

God: Imagine yourself in My position, Blake. Imagine someone speaking foolishness and lies while representing you. Would you not wish that person could muster enough good sense to shut up? I'm not excusing folly done in My name. Rather, I am cautioning you not to become swayed by appearance. Don't make surface judgments—about television evangelists or someone like Katie.

Blake7: I'm glad we are back to Katie because I have a question: I love it that Jesus chose rogues, tax collectors, and "sinners" as His friends, His disciples even. He didn't hang with the rich, the powerful, and the beautiful. But . . .

God: Yes?

Blake7: Well, doesn't the Bible say that bad company corrupts good character?

CrossKrys: Blake, you're asking GOD what the Bible says? Hello??? Duh!

God: ☺

Blake7: OK, that was a dumb question. But at least it made someone smile. But I still think I have a point. How do you befriend hard kids, kids who are ghetto, and not be corrupted by them?

God: Blake, I commend you for your careful thought and study of My Word. I'm going to make this one easy for you: As you seek to befriend people like those My Son reached out to, ask yourself, *Why am I pursuing this relationship?* When Jesus reached out to Zaccheus, He knew exactly what He was doing and why He was doing it. Also, constantly examine where the friendship is taking those involved. Are you drawing your friends closer to Me, or are they pulling you away from Me?

CrossKrys: Yeah! Good point!

God: Why, thank you!

CrossKrys: I am just totally feeling what you are saying. It's like, I love Katie. I love hanging with her. But I'm not into what she's into. I'm not gonna get high with her. I'm not going to get into a car driven by one of her drunk friends. I'm so not about that! I'm not going to lose sight of common sense. And she totally respects that. Sure, she asked me to burn a blunt with her a couple of times, but once she saw I wasn't into that, she was cool about it.

Blake7: Krys, you rock!

CrossKrys: Yeah, now all I have to do is figure out what it is that I am into, and who it is that I am. So far, all I've figured out is who I'm NOT.

JennSmiles: Yo, kids, maybe we can figure that one out next time, huh? I'm fadin'.

Blake7: You've been pretty quiet up till now, Jenn. Did you nap on us?

JennSmiles: Nah. I know I haven't been Chatty Kathy, but that doesn't mean I haven't been pondering.

Blake7: You've been pondering?

JennSmiles: Yeah. So what? I have been known to ponder occasionally. It doesn't mean I'm ready to join a church. And it doesn't mean I'm convinced that this whole God-in-the-Chat-Room thing isn't a big joke or some kinda Christian commando tactic you cooked up, Blake. So don't get the wrong idea.

Blake7: Does this feel like a joke, a tactical ploy? Be honest.

JennSmiles: Well . . . no. That's why I've been doing so much pondering. And as for Jesus, any guy who hung with crooks and hookers and cheesed off the holier-than-thou types is OK in my book.

God: He fares well in My book too.

JennSmiles: OK, then. It's nice to end on a positive note. Now, all of you, scram, please. Except you, Krys. I'm gonna get a Dr. Pepper, then I want to talk to you ALONE for just a bit before I visit Dreamland.

CrossKrys: OK, go obey your thirst, Jenn. Talk to you in a few.

Blake7: Yeah, Krys's advice is good, Jenn. Just remember to obey more than just physical thirsts.

JennSmiles: Whatever. Goodnight, men. A fond goodnight, I mean.

****

Private Chat #108:

Just the Two of Us

 Participants Here: 2
JennSmiles · CrossKrys

JennSmiles: Hey.

CrossKrys: Hey indeed. You OK?

JennSmiles: Yeah. Are things OK at school for you? The rumor stuff dying down?

CrossKrys: It is, actually. There's always some juicier gossip around the corner. One of the coaches allegedly "inappropriately touched" a girl on the basketball team. That's the new scandal for the week. I'm kinda old news. I am glad you haven't made the mistakes I have.

JennSmiles: Well, I've made plenty that even you don't know about. But I guess we've made different ones.

CrossKrys: Well, just be careful out there. Don't listen to the lies. Don't listen to all the smack that guys talk. So, she says as she changes the subject, how long have your parentals been divorced? I forgot.

JennSmiles: Let's see . . . about a year since it became final and official and all that. Yours split just before we started chatting last summer, right?

CrossKrys: Righto. It's nice to have someone who can relate to what it's like to have divorced parents. It makes me feel close to you.

JennSmiles: I'm glad. I mean, I'm glad we are here for each other, not that your parents split.

CrossKrys: . . . or that your parents split, right?

JennSmiles: Yeah. Right.

CrossKrys: Are you OK?

JennSmiles: Yeah, just a little tired, I guess.

CrossKrys: Do you wanna talk about him?

JennSmiles: Him who? God?

CrossKrys: Well, not right now. I was referring to Blake.

JennSmiles: That's good, because I don't want to talk about God right now. It brings up too many questions and problems, and I will lie awake all night pondering and stuff. I need my beauty sleep. Heaven knows that's true.

CrossKrys: Puh-leeze. We gotta work on your self-esteem. You probably blame yourself for your parentals' divorce,

world hunger, and the hole in the
ozone to boot, don't ya?

JennSmiles: That ozone hole—I have nothing
to do with that. I use roll-on
deodorant, I'll have you know.

CrossKrys: So, anyway, back to Blake. I have
been wanting to ask you, do you
like him?

JennSmiles: I don't know. Why are you asking?
Do YOU like him? Are you
smitten, kitten?

CrossKrys: Maybe. Maybe I'm a little smitten.
But I'm not in deep smit. Now it's
your turn . . .

JennSmiles: To tell you the truth . . . you know,
I don't know how I feel. How do
you want me to feel?

CrossKrys: What kind of question is that? You
can feel anyway you want to.

JennSmiles: No need to jump on me, K. I was just trying to be considerate. You know, maybe we shouldn't talk about this particular topic.

CrossKrys: OK, if that's what you want.

JennSmiles: It's what I want. In fact, I don't want to talk about anything right now. I gotta bounce. Laterz.

CrossKrys: Jenn?

CrossKrys: Jenn? You there? Hmmm. Well, that was interesting.

****

Private Chat #109:

Secrets, Lies, & Alibis

Participants Here: 5
God · Blake7 · CrossKrys · JennSmiles · A.C.008

JennSmiles: Well, since we're all here, I have something to tell you. I've been thinking a lot about this, so nobody interrupt me, OK!

CrossKrys: You have wide-open screen; Jenn, go for it.

JennSmiles: OK, this is hard, but . . . here goes. I need to leave our little clique. For good, I suppose. You all are going one direction. I can't go that way. I feel us getting closer, but—and hear this, Blake—it's getting closer around GOD. And that's just not

131

for me. I just can't do this God thing. I'm not who you think I am.

Blake7: Jenn, is it OK to talk now?

JennSmiles: Shoot.

Blake7: Jenn, please don't leave us. We care. I care. And yes, I'll admit it, I pray every night that you'll let God be in your life. But I'm your friend, no matter what. Always.

JennSmiles: You are just saying that. You could never let the God-thing go. I know you. Onward, little Christian soldier.

Blake7: Jenn, listen. You are NOT some religious conquest to me. You're right, in a way. I'll never stop caring about you, body and soul. Especially soul. And I'll never stop talking about my faith. Jesus is the only Hero I have in this world. I will never hide who I am. But, I promise you, I'm your friend forever, no matter what. As God is my Witness—literally.

CrossKrys: My turn now, my friend. I am, like, heartbroken and PO'd at the same time. How can you talk about ditching us? Is this why you cut our conversation so short the other night? What is up? I have told you things I haven't told my own sister or any of my friends at school. In so many ways, you are my closest friend. Why are you talking like this?

JennSmiles: I am sooooo sorry, Krys. You have been nothing but an angel to me. I just don't fit with this group, OK? I have wanted to fit with you, but it's not working.

A.C.OO8: Personally, I think you should do whatever you want, Jenn. But I'm curious. Why do you think YOU don't fit? You think I blend with this crew? But still, I'm here. I'm not sure why. I'm not sure for how long. But I'm here.

JennSmiles: At least you are honest about who you are, Ace. And I think you could take this clique or leave it. Maybe you're here just cuz you're bored. But this group means so much to me. And I've ruined it.

Blake7: What do you mean?

JennSmiles: OK, I'm crying now. And I hate that. When I'm in these chats, it's like the only time I cry. The rest of the time, I'm numb. You guys, I wanted you to accept me so bad. And . . . well . . . I have lied to you. A lot.

CrossKrys: About what, Jenn? It seems like you shoot pretty straight. Please tell me

you are not a forty-five-year-old
man who still lives with his parents
or a fifty-two-year-old bar hag . . .

CrossKrys: Jenn? Please answer!

JennSmiles: OK. OK. Just give me a minute. I
gotta find a Kleenex.

Blake7: We'll wait . . .

****

Private Chat #109:

Secrets, Lies, & Alibis, Version 2.0

Participants Here: 5
God · JennSmiles · CrossKrys · A.C.008 · Blake7

JennSmiles: I'm back and de-snotted now. To your question, Krys, no, it's nothing like that. I'm not a middle-aged perv or a bar hag. I've been straight with you about my gender, age, locale, all that stuff. And every feeling I've expressed has been real. From my heart. But there have been so many times when I've wanted this group's sympathy. But other times I craved your approval. I didn't want to be the one who was always the screw-up. I wanted to dish advice from the high road. So, I've adjusted my life story accordingly.

CrossKrys: <stunned> Adjusted? In what ways?

JennSmiles: For starters, my parentals aren't
divorced. I just thought saying that
made me sound sympathetic and so
very 21st century. I lied. They do
hate each other. It's either scream-o-
rama or a total freeze-out in the old
Lindsay household.

Blake7:   What else, Jenn? What else don't we
know about the real you?

JennSmiles: Oh, gosh, where do I begin? Well,
here's one for ya, B. Remember that
e-mail I sent you a month ago—
when I said I was still a virgin?
Nope. Not true. In fact, I was "not
a virgin" again at a party last week.
And here's the kicker: I told you I
had a boyfriend for a long time.
Nope. Nada. No boyfriend. Never
had one. Just an occasional boy.
You see, I can find guys who want

to hook up with me, no problem. I
just can't find one to love me.

Blake7: Maybe you're looking in the
wrong places.

JennSmiles: Or maybe love is a lie. Look at all
the divorces. Look at the crap-
marriages like my parents'. I
wonder how many couples are just
like Al and Terri Lindsay. Just
sticking together "for the sake of
the children"? Or for the sake of
their reputations? Or maybe they're
just too lazy to get divorced. Or it's
not financially prudent.

CrossKrys: Jenn, I don't care about the lies.
Sure, I'm hurt. But as long as you
are still YOU, we can do this. I
wish you felt that you could be
yourself with me, but maybe we can
work on that. And it's not as if
you've murdered an orphan or

drowned a bunch o' puppies. You just told a few lies. BTW, were you lying about your acne problem?

JennSmiles: No, my zits are only too real. I'll never be a Cover Girl. I lied the first time we ever talked, when I told you that the guys at school say I look kinda like Jessica Simpson. Nobody has ever said that to me. I just wish someone would. I got my hair cut like hers and everything. But to most of the guys at school I might as well be BART Simpson.

Blake7: I have an idea. Let's promise each other we'll tell the truth from now on. No matter how it makes us look. No matter if it might offend someone. We must be able to trust each other. I thought we could before, but at least we can start now. What do you say, group?

A.C.008: Whatever, B-man. It's not like I give a rip what any of you think of me—or each other—anyway.

Blake7: What about the rest of you?

God: I think you know where I stand on truth, Blake.

CrossKrys: I'm in, B. BTW, I might have exaggerated a few times, but I've basically been straight with y'all. So, see, Jenn, we all stretch the truth sometime (deities excepted, Mr. God Sir). We can get past this. There's no permanent damage.

JennSmiles: <sigh of frustration> Krys! Hear me! You can't fix this. You all are good people, even you, Ace. You're a total stoner, but you wouldn't harm a fly. And you're really not so aloof as you put on. Remember, you're dealing with a master of deception here. Anyway, back to my point, cuz I do have one: You all have good hearts. You are loving people. I can feel you being drawn to the center of this circle. With God there in the middle. I can feel you all changing.

Blake7: But on this journey toward God, Jenn, we want you with us. We need you with us.

JennSmiles: And therein swims the fly in the Fruit Loops, Blake. I ain't coming with you! My heart isn't the same as yours. Mine is one giant callous. Don't you get it? I don't WANT to be close to God. I'm not supposed to be. I don't want to go to heaven and munch angel food cake and play the harp forever and ever. I will not sit in a circle and hold hands with my neighbors and sing "Kum Ba Yah."

CrossKrys: Jenn, I'm confused; you're talking about God and heaven as if you believe in them. What happened to my l'il atheist?

JennSmiles: Score one for Inspector Krys! You just sniffed out another lie! Surprise! I'm not an atheist. How do you like them kumquats? See, I know God is real. It's just that I'm not cut out to hang with him. I did used to be an atheist, though, for real.

Blake7: God, we seem to be at a loss here. Please help.

God: Jennifer, tell us why you don't see Me and My heavenly kingdom in your future?

JennSmiles: OK, but let's get one thing straight first: I believe there's a God. I'm not sure it's you, whoever you are in this chat room. But maybe you are God. Or maybe you're just some

computer genius, bedazzling us
with Jedi mind tricks. Krys, how'd
you like that word—"bedazzling?"
I'm trying to get smart like you. I'm
learning a new word a day.

Blake7: Don't try to change the subject, Jenn.
There's a question on the screen . . .

JennSmiles: Fair enough, B. Let's see, why aren't
God and heaven and all that in my
future? Hmmm. Let's see. Could it
be because I don't WANT God in
my future? Could it be because I
know my own heart? Or, drum roll
please, could it be that I don't love
God? Sometimes I wish I did. But I
don't. I don't want to serve God. I
don't want my life to revolve
around him. I don't want to be
obligated to God or anyone else.

Blake7: Jenn . . .

JennSmiles: Shut and let me finish, B. Listen, I have known since I was fourteen that I was a sinner who's going to hell the hard way. I know it in my heart. I know it in my mind. And, you, here in the chat, if you are truly God, then you know all this. I don't love you. I'm a bad seed. I'm a liar. If there's a door marked Evil Inside: Step Right This Way, you know I'm sprinting through it. I can't help myself.

Blake7: Jenn, please stop. You're not a bad seed. And despite the lies, we've gotten to know you pretty well over these past months. You are not evil. You are not a bad person.

CrossKrys: Ditto that, Jenn!

JennSmiles: You guys don't know my heart. But you do, don't you, God? You know what I have confessed here tonight is true. And you probably know a few things I've done, which I have never told anyone before. And I'll bet you know the last name of the guy I was with last Saturday. Cuz gosh-darn-it, all I can remember is "Tom." When I think about it all, I cry until my eyes swell shut. I can't stand to be this way, but I can't help myself. I AM a bad seed. So, go ahead, God. Butch me. Send some fire and brimstone down from heaven. Or, I know, I'll put my hands on the keyboard, and you can electrocute me! Come on, God. I'm waitin'. Put me out of my misery. Or leave me alone. But give it up. I'm not one of yours.

God: Jenn, how could I give up on you? My heart turns against it. Before I formed you in the womb, I knew you. Let Me love you now. Let Me hold you close, as a mother holds an infant against her cheek. Destroy you, Jennifer? Abandon you? My heart recoils from it. My whole being trembles at even the thought of it. I have no wish to destroy you. I am Love, and I love you. And as for your heart, I will give you a new heart and put a new spirit in you. I will remove your heart of stone and give you a heart of flesh. I know you have a broken heart. I want to give you a new one.

CrossKrys: Oh my God, that was beautiful.

God: Thank you. Look at the words on your screen, Jennifer. Understand their truth. Feel their power. Feel their healing. All of you, read My words; this is My message for you. This is My unrelenting stance toward you: I love you.

JennSmiles: I have this niece. She's eighteen months old. I hold her against my cheek, just like you said. Her skin is so soft. And she looks so happy when I hold her like that in front of a mirror. I feel so much love for her. It's one of the only pure moments in my whole stupid life. And you say it's like that, God, with you and me? It just can't be real. I can't be loved like that.

God: You can be. You are.

JennSmiles: Me? You gotta be kidding. Would you swear to that on your own Bible? Would you stake your life on that?

God: A while ago, I became human bones and flesh, in the form of My Son. I walked around on your planet. Your dirt. I was beaten and ridiculed. Then I died for the sake of love. I died for you, Jennifer. Stake my life on it? I already have.

CrossKrys: Jenn, that is so awesome. Are you hearing this? Are you feeling this?

Blake7: Jenn? Are you here?

CrossKrys: I guess she's gone.

A.C.008: What do we do now? This seems like one of those "This is a job for Superman" times or something.

God: No, it's a job for Me.

****

February 10

Private Chat #110:

A Room Called Despair

 Participants Here: 2
JennSmiles · God

JennSmiles: I am alone. It figures. The others were supposed to be here at 10. Why am I even typing this?

God: Excuse me?

JennSmiles: Oh, you. Guess I didn't see your name up there.

God: Common mistake. But I'm always around. Even in a Room Called Despair.

JennSmiles: Well then, how come in the past I have called out for answers, and

149

nobody gave me jack? Not you. Not anyone.

God: I always have the answers. I just don't always hand them to you on a platter. Some answers you discover, you learn, you piece together bit by bit. It takes time to become wise.

JennSmiles: Well, actually, I am hoping for an answer from you now. A friend of mine is considering suicide. I am really worried about her.

God: I am listening.

JennSmiles: Well, what should I tell her?

God: You think you need to talk her out of it?

JennSmiles: What kind of answer is that? Don't you care if she dies?

God: Yes, I do. But I created her with a free will.

JennSmiles: So she can overdose on Valium if she wants to, right?

God: Yes, some people do that.

JennSmiles: But what about her life?

God: Her life is always in My hands, but the choices about that life are in hers. The real problem is not whether she keeps breathing or walking around on Earth. What truly matters is whether she accepts Me or not. That's a choice that matters for eternity.

JennSmiles: Oh, yeah, that's right. You religious types all think we live forever. But what if you're wrong?

God: You don't believe there is a heavenly life beyond your planet, the earthly existence you experience?

151

JennSmiles: No, I don't. You have a bit of time here. You search for love. You search for hope. You don't find them. You allow yourself to become vulnerable with people. You pour out your heart; then you wish you could take it all back. You are humiliated. You can't face people again. You can't face yourself one more day. And even if you can find the strength to press on, to live, what's the point? You get old. Your hair gets wiry. Your skin sags. Your bones become brittle. Your mind starts to fail you. Then you're gone. A few somber guys in suits carry your sad old carcass into a hearse; then they put you in the ground. Why wait around for that? That's why my friend is so bummed. It's like, what's the point? I know just how she feels. You try so hard to be happy, but then reality hits you. It would be nice to think of an eternal paradise, but I just don't believe it. Hell? That I can picture. Heaven? No way.

God: What if you're wrong?

JennSmiles: What do you mean?

God: What do you think will happen if you overdose?

JennSmiles: Well . . . hey, we're not talking about me. It's my friend who needs help!

God: Really? If you say so.

JennSmiles: How could you know any differently? Oh, yeah, you're probably going to give me some line about knowing everything.

God: What do you think that I know?

JennSmiles: Quit stalling. What should I tell my friend?

God: Tell her I love her. I will always love her—even if she decides to destroy herself. Ask her what the world will be missing if she leaves it. Ask her who will do the good works I have planned for her. Ask her who will receive all the blessings I want to give her while she is on this earth. Remind her that she's a one-of-a-kind work of My hands. Ask her if there is something she should try before she tries suicide.

JennSmiles: What if she has tried everything else?

God: She hasn't tried Me. I am the Answer. Without Me, she doesn't have life. With Me, she will ALWAYS have it.

JennSmiles: Even if she kills herself?

God: If the lonely, empty place inside her is filled with My love, she won't feel like dying. She'll feel like living. I have created every person with a purpose. Some people disregard that purpose. But if you will open your eyes and discover that you are loved, that you matter to Me, and that the world needs you, you will find hope.

JennSmiles: You mean SHE will find hope.

God: If you say so.

JennSmiles: Well, I guess what you have said is worth thinking about. I'm not saying I buy it all, but I think my friend and I should talk about this.

God: I think so too. Please remind your friend that I love her. Let's talk again soon.

JennSmiles: Will do, sir. Thank you. And I know my friend would want me to thank you too.

God: You are both welcome.

****

February 17

Private Chat #111:

The Mountaintop

 Participants Here: 2
God · Blake 7

Blake7: I am so glad it's just the two of us tonight, Sir.

God: Why is that?

Blake7: I have questions that I'm afraid to ask in front of the others.

God: Why?

Blake7: Well, I'm sorry, but sometimes I doubt. Sometimes there are things I don't understand. But I don't want to spook the others, you know? Don't want to trip them up.

157

Especially Jenn. She's in such a
vulnerable position.

God: I understand. But I have a question
for you. Do you believe that the
Bible is My Word? That I inspired
people to write it?

Blake7: Yes.

God: And I know you've read the Psalms.

Blake7: I love the Psalms!

God: Why do you think I inspired David
and other psalmists to question Me?
To express their despair, frustration,
even anger?

Blake7: Uh . . .

Blake7: I guess I never thought of it that
way: You, actually inspiring people
to question Your ways openly
and passionately.

God: What does this show you about Me?

Blake7: Why are You making this so hard? Why can't You just explain it all?

God: Is that really what you want? To be force-fed life's wisdom until you bloat? Or would you rather take a bite out of it through your own choice—to chew it, savor it, digest it? Oh, Blake, when will you learn that life is meant to be discovered and enjoyed one moment at a time? You climbed Pikes Peak last summer.

Blake7: Yes, Sir, I did. But I'm missing the segue. What does that have to do with our conversation?

God: How did you feel when you finally reached the summit of that mountain, after six hours of climbing?

Blake7: Tired, relieved. But also triumphant. Like I'd really accomplished something. I looked back down the mountain at how far I'd come. It rocked, actually.

God: What if you had been magically transported from the foot of the mountain to the summit in less than a second? Would you have felt the same way about yourself and your journey? Would you have felt you had accomplished anything?

Blake7: Okay, you got me.

God: That I do. Now, as to My question about the Psalms . . .

Blake7: Well, I guess that if you confront your doubts and confusion and express them openly, you are actually dealing with them. Not minimizing them or pretending they don't exist.

God: And can you ever conquer something by pretending it's not there?

Blake7: I see what You mean. But what
about Krys, A.C., and Jenn? What
will they think of me if they see
that I doubt, just as they do? They
seem to rely on me a lot. I don't
want to turn them away from You.
It's a lot of pressure. And, Jenn, Sir.
I have to be strong for her even
more than the others . . .

God: Blake, you asked what they will
think of you if you share doubt.
What if they think you are a real
person, with real emotions, real
doubts, real questions? What would
be wrong with that?

Blake7: Nothing, I guess. But I want them
to love You. To have faith. I don't
want to stand in the way. As I said,
the pressure of it all, it feels like it's

going to crush me sometimes. I care about them so much.

God: Blake, which one of us is God?

Blake7: That would be You, Sir.

God: Yes. And their souls are in good hands, Mine. You have prayed for them. I have heard those prayers. You have reached out to them. I am pleased with you. Just don't try to carry the weight you weren't meant to carry.

Blake7: OK.

God: Remember that I will give you rest when you are weary and burdened. Rest well tonight, Blake. Krys, A.C., and Jennifer have a true friend in you.

Blake7: A friend loves at all times. I read that somewhere.

God: Yes, it sounds quite familiar to Me. Goodnight, My son.

Blake7: Goodnight, um, Dad. May I call You that?

God: I like it. I have been called many names today. None better than Dad.

****

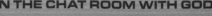
Private Chat #112:

The Way It Was

Participants Here: 2
JennSmiles · CrossKrys

JennSmiles: Well, it's just the two of us. Just like in the beginning. I need some time with just you again; you know what I mean?

CrossKrys: Yep. Remember how we met in that Romantic Rendez-Vous room last summer? You stuck up for me when that guy was harassing me.

JennSmiles: That I did. He was a zipper-head. It's weird; that night was the one-month anniversary of my breakup with my imaginary boyfriend, Cam. I was looking for romance. I found a friend instead. You've been a way

better friend than Cam ever was.
Or any of the real guys I've met.
What is up with guys today? Do
they all take selfish 'n' stupid pills?

CrossKrys: Not all of 'em. There is, of course,
Blake.

JennSmiles: I wonder what he looks like. He
doesn't have a pic scanned.

CrossKrys: If he looks as fine as his personality
. . . whoa baby! But even if he is a
Herb, he'd still be a good friend.

JennSmiles: He IS a good friend. Unless . . .

CrossKrys: Unless?

JennSmiles: Unless he's using us. Maybe he's got
one of his church buddies playing
God. Maybe he's just messing with
our heads.

CrossKrys: I have wondered that. I have
wondered if Blake has some adult

helping him. 'Cuz whoever that God persona is, he's saying stuff I don't think a teen could come up with—even a churchified teen. Maybe it's Blake's dad.

JennSmiles: Please don't yuck me out.

CrossKrys: But here's what gets me: Why? Why would Blake set up this big charade? What's in it for him? He's not scamming on us. He isn't vying for phone sex or cyber sex. He isn't trying to get our credit card numbers or passwords and rip us off. Come on, we're smart girls. We've been burned enough times. We both know that guys can't hide their hidden agendas for long.

JennSmiles: Yeah, a guy can't pull the wool over this little lamb's eyes. Unless he's really hot.

CrossKrys: ☺ And maybe Blake is hot, who knows? Maybe he's caliente! But the point is, here's this guy who spends hours with us every week, and he doesn't want anything in return. Do you realize he's never asked to see our pics—even though he knows we both have them? So he doesn't even know how gorgeous we are.

JennSmiles: Speak for yourself.

CrossKrys: Come on, Jenn. You're totally cute.

JennSmiles: Yeah, right. I hate my hair. I hate my skin. This morning I looked in the mirror and said, "It's official. I am now the ugliest person I know."

CrossKrys: Are not! But even if you were, I don't think that would matter to Blake.

JennSmiles: Maybe you're right. Is this a scenario or what? We are friends with either the world's nicest guy or the world's best liar. Or make that two liars: Blake and his pretending-to-be-God cohort.

CrossKrys: Unless . . . it really is God.

JennSmiles: Come on, Krys. This dude on the computer doesn't match what I've heard of God.

CrossKrys: Maybe that's because the real God isn't who all the movie makers, politicians, philosophers, and TV preachers have made him out to be. Maybe in reality he's more like . . . himself. I like it that he doesn't pop out sweet little answers like candy from a Pez dispenser. He helps us think. He makes us wonder. Besides, you sure seemed convinced the other night. Remember?

JennSmiles: Hmmm . . . Well, that's true. And he is so nice to us. I had always pictured God as this way-harsh old man. I'm not ready to swallow all of this religion stuff, but he does make me feel worth something.

CrossKrys: Right. Me too. And besides, if God isn't all about love, how do you explain a guy like Blake? How do you explain all the talks we've had—how close we've become? And how come God and Blake both ask us questions so huge that I can barely wrap my brain around them?

JennSmiles: And you have some brain on ya, Miss 4.0.

CrossKrys: Gosh, thanks. My cerebellum is blushing. But back to big questions: I have another one for you. If there is no loving God in this world, how do you explain how I've found a perfect friend on the Internet—the world's biggest gathering place for playas, Herbs, and liars? I don't think it was an accident that I met you. I think maybe it was a Godsend.

JennSmiles: If you make me cry, I'm gonna smack you up. Quit talking nice.

CrossKrys: OK, you warthog.

JennSmiles: That's better. Witch.

CrossKrys: Skrod.

JennSmiles: Cow.

CrossKrys: Bad seed.

JennSmiles: Soul mate.

CrossKrys: Friend 4 Life.

JennSmiles: Don't ever quit being my friend. I will whup your sorry butt. Oh man, I am so tired. I didn't mean to keep you this long tonight. It's 2 a.m. I can't believe it.

CrossKrys: You can keep me as long as you want.

JennSmiles: Goodnight. And I am so NOT crying now.

CrossKrys: If you say so.

****

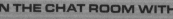
Private Chat #113:

Only the Young Die Good

Participants Here: 4
CrossKrys · JennSmiles · Blake7 · God

JennSmiles: Wow, it's been a couple weeks since we've talked. What's been goin' on?

CrossKrys: You guys, I am so shredded. Four nights ago, some kids from our school went hill-jumping, and it was bad news. That's why I haven't been online for a while.

JennSmiles: Hill-jumping? You mean where they zoom over a hill in a car so they can catch mad air?

CrossKrys: Yeah. But they caught too much mad air. The driver lost control when his car hit the pavement.

They lost the road and hit a tree. This fourteen-year-old girl, the driver's cousin, she DIED! I still can't believe it. She was the only one not wearing a seatbelt.

Blake7: I am so sorry, Krys.

CrossKrys: Thanks. It's like there's a dark cloud over our whole school, our whole town.

JennSmiles: What about the other people in the car? How are they? Do you know them well?

CrossKrys: Our high school is small, only 400 of us. I know almost everybody. The four people in the car weren't good friends of mine, but still. . . . It's like something has invaded us. The other three are still in the hospital. God, why do people have to get hurt? Why do some die so young? Please help me understand why this had to happen. This girl, Beth, she was really sweet. She was really popular in the freshman class. She was on Student Council with me.

God: We have talked before about the pain we endure for the sake of freedom.

Blake7: Yeah, even kids abuse their freedom in tragic ways.

CrossKrys: I guess so, but that's not helping me! My heart is dying because of this! I don't feel safe anymore. I guess I used to assume I would live a long, long time. Now, I realize that might not be the case. And at the same time I'm bumming, I'm also furious. Kids around here have been hill-jumping since I was a little kid, probably longer. And every few years, there's a serious injury. Or someone dies. Then the adults all wring their hands and shake their heads. There are editorials and letters to the editor in our weekly paper. We have assemblies where the principal and a highway patrol officer warn and threaten everybody. We all cry. But we don't learn. We never seem to learn. . . .

God, please tell me that Beth is OK.

God: Blake, please read Luke 18:16-17 for us, especially for my daughter Krys.

Blake7: "Jesus called the children to him and said, 'Let the little children come to me, and do not hinder them, for the kingdom of God belongs to such as these. I tell you the truth, anyone who will not

receive the kingdom of God like a
little child will never enter it.'"

God: Those are the words of My Son.
He once walked the earth as a
child, as a teen.

Blake7: See, Krys? God loves kids. Beth was
just a kid. A fourteen-year-old kid.

CrossKrys: Her poor parents. She was an only
child. I liked Beth's laugh. It
sounded like a little machine gun or
something. Please, God, tell me
you'll take care of her.

God: I will take care of her. My kingdom
is full of kids. If you could see them
right now, could you dare to believe
your own eyes? No one shows joy
like a child.

Blake7: Yeah, you should see the kids in our
junior church when I surprise them
by bringing them little Snickers

bars or Laffy Taffy. Man, I love how they squeal and scream and jump around—and shove that candy into their mouths in one bite! They know how to enjoy stuff.

CrossKrys: Mr. God Sir, will there be Snickers bars in heaven? I'd like to think of Beth munching on one right now.

God: Let Me put it this way, Krys. There is much here that is sweet to the body and to the soul.

CrossKrys: That is good to know. But we are going to miss Beth. And the other three; they were hurt pretty bad. It will take them a long time to heal.

God: The driver was intoxicated. More than his body will need to heal.

CrossKrys: I don't know how he's going to live with what happened. It's going to haunt him forever. I think his life is ruined, to be honest.

God: Perhaps not. My grace and forgiveness can work wonders. There's a fellow up here named Paul. You should ask him about this someday.

JennSmiles: Paul who?

Blake7: Jenn, Paul was this radical intellectual who used to bust on Christians. He persecuted them. Harassed them. Even approved their being brutally murdered for their faith in Jesus.

God: Then one day, he met Jesus personally.

Blake7: Yep. He was dumbstruck. He was blinded, and I mean literally. Jesus asked him, "Why are you persecuting Me?"

JennSmiles: Wait a sec. Was this Paul dude doing stuff to Jesus?

Blake7: No. Not exactly. That is just how closely Jesus identifies with His people. Check this out: Jesus has said that He will reward people for feeding the hungry, clothing the naked, visiting the sick and the imprisoned. He says in Matthew 25:40, "I tell you the truth, whatever you did for one of the least of these brothers of mine, you did for me." Think about that: It's not, "It's just like doing something for Me." It's flat-out, "You did it for Me." It's beyond empathy. It's beyond anything we can understand. If we help others, we help Jesus. And, Krys, when we hurt, He hurts.

CrossKrys: I never knew that. It's hard to imagine Jesus identifying with a homeless derelict, a criminal in prison, or some sickly person in a Red Cross Shelter. Or a heartbroken parent.

JennSmiles: That is deep. If it's true, that is.

God: Jenn, do you think any of us is lying to you?

JennSmiles: I don't know. I guess not. It's just . . . I'm still trying to figure out who you REALLY are.

God: Who do you think I am?

JennSmiles: I just don't KNOW! And that's why I can get no peace lately. These conversations stick to me like gum on the bottom of my shoe. Sometimes I wish we'd never met. Life was simpler before.

Blake7: Come on, Jenn. Life was simpler when you were a newborn too. Eat.

Poop. Sleep. But was your life richer and fuller then? Would you like to go back?

JennSmiles: Maybe. Sometimes. You were talking earlier about becoming like a child.

Blake7: Jenn, don't con a con. There's a difference between child-like and child-ish, or infantile.

CrossKrys: Yeah, Jenn, I'm calling smoke on you. You're totally blowing smoke.

JennSmiles: OK. I'm busted, I guess. But I still can't reason this out. God stands by while these kids play Demolition Derby; then he welcomes the victims into heaven? I just can't get past the idea of someone watching people hurt themselves. But, on the other hand, no one loves freedom more than I do. Even if it's the freedom to screw up my life. I'm glad I have the choice.

CrossKrys: Well, I guess Beth's life is screwed up. God, can she see us now?

God: Beth can see all that she needs to see to be perfectly happy. What do you all think that means?

Blake7: I don't think people in Heaven can see us. The book of Revelation says that in Heaven there are no tears, no sorrows. And if people could see their loved ones on earth, they would miss them. They'd feel sorrow. Right, God?

God: You are assuming that people in Heaven still see things from an earthly perspective. Do you not think that things are different in Heaven? Right now, on earth, can you see and hear your loved ones? And can you be aware of them even when you can't communicate with them?

Blake7: Sure, of course I can.

God: Do you think that in Heaven you will see less than you see now? Or more? Will you be less aware? Or more?

CrossKrys: OK, I'm pullin' a brain muscle here. I just can't handle all of this right now. God, please just assure me that Beth is OK. That she is healed and warm and safe and loved.

God: She is all of those things and more. You have My Word on that.

CrossKrys: Thank you.

God: You are welcome. Jenn and Blake, Krys needs some time now. Away from a computer screen. Away from almost everything. Except Me.

CrossKrys: How did you know I was thinki . . .
<blushing> Oh, yeah. Never mind.

JennSmiles: He's right, Krys. We'll step off. Go
someplace quiet. Cry your eyes out.
Punch something if you need to.
And you have my phone number,
so call me if you need to.

Blake7: I'll e-mail you my number, too,
Krys. Just in case.

God: And you have My number. I'm in
the Book.

CrossKrys: ☺ I can't believe someone could
make me smile at a time like this. I
just might talk to you later, Mr.
God Sir.

God: ☺ Now you made Me smile.
One thing before you all go . . .

CrossKrys: Yes?

God: My children, be careful how you live. Be wise. Be mindful of your freedom and of the freedom of others. Respect yourselves. Take care of one another, just as you have been doing. Goodnight.

JennSmiles: Hey, his name is not on the top of the screen anymore. Look.

CrossKrys: You know, he sounded kind of sad.

Blake7: I think He's sad about Beth.

CrossKrys: But if Beth is in heaven, she's not sad, right? She's not hurting anymore.

Blake7: I don't think He is sad over Beth, directly. I think He's sad for you, Krys, and for all the people who love her. Especially her parents. God knows what it's like to lose an only child to a violent death.

CrossKrys: Hey, that's right. Maybe he really does understand how we all feel. Maybe I will try to talk to him, and not on the computer. It's been a long time since I prayed.

Blake7: Well, I will be praying for you, Krys. Let me know how your talk with God goes, if you decide to pray.

CrossKrys: Will do. What about you, my l'il sometimes-atheist? Will you say a prayer for me?

JennSmiles: I'll have a good thought for you. How's that? That's the best I can do right now.

Blake7: Jenn, it's a start.

CrossKrys: Yeah, it's a start. Thanks, Jenn. I'll have a good thought for you too. And maybe a prayer.

JennSmiles: That's cool with me. Couldn't hurt. But focus on you. Take time to heal. And let's talk again soon, kids. Laterz.

****

Private Chat #114:

The Rap on Rep

 Participants Here: 4
JennSmiles · CrossKrys · Blake7 · God

JennSmiles: Yo, I can't believe it's been so long since we talked. I guess everyone else has been as mad-busy as I was. Where have y'all been?

God: Here, there, and everywhere.

CrossKrys: Well, I can't match that, but it has been test-o-rama time at my l'il high school in the wild, wild west.

Blake7: Went to Arizona for spring break. And track practice has started. I've been running fifty miles a week. I am loving it.

188

JennSmiles: Loving running? As I have said before, B, you are a freak of nature. Speaking of freaks, has anybody heard from Ace?

CrossKrys: Nope.

Blake7: Nada here as well.

JennSmiles: Weird. He usually e-mails me at least once a week. And I've e-mailed him like ten times, but no answer. I hope he's OK.

CrossKrys: God, can you tell us what's up with him? Can we do anything for him?

God: Pray for him.

Blake7: Will do, Sir.

CrossKrys: Yeah, ditto that. I hope he comes back. But, and I hate to be a pest, can't you please tell us what's up with him?

God: He's at war.

JennSmiles: Ace joined the army? Nah, he'd never pass the drug tes . . . Oh, delete that. I get it. It's like a personal war, right?

Blake7: I bet he's struggling to do the right thing. I am glad he's at least putting up a fight. We should totally pray for him.

God: Yes, that's a fine suggestion.

CrossKrys: Hcy, could you guys pray for me, too (quasi-atheists excluded—Jenn!)

Blake7: Sure, Krys. What's up?

CrossKrys: Well, I've been going to a church youth group once in a while. Blake helped me find this cool church via the Net. Anyway, word has gotten out. (In our school, everybody knows what you have for breakfast!)

And it's weird; people are treating me differently. Some of the seniors are calling me "one of the creeps for Christ." Stuff like that. It bites! Even some of my friends are acting all spooky around me, like I've joined a cult or something. I admit; it stings. I've gone from being at least sorta cool to a total leper.

Blake7: First, congratulations, Krys! I'm so glad you checked out that church. My youth pastor knows yours. But, back to the subject at hand: I hear ya, Krys. Christians aren't the coolest people at my school either. No one really calls us names, but I catch people staring at me after I pray over my food in the cafeteria. And several teachers are famous for talking about all the wars and atrocities committed in the name of God. And they always make fun of political figures or actors who promote prayer in school, creationism over evolution, stuff like that.

CrossKrys: Yeah, that happens at my school too. But, and please don't take offense, Mr. God Sir, I've noticed something about the Christians at school. You see, they're mostly, uh, Herbs. I mean, compared to them I AM way cool. What's up with that? Why do Christians talk in religious cliches, band together in these tight little cliques, and buy all their clothes at Super Target? I'm sorry, but do they think Abercrombie & Fitch are the devil's brothers or what?

Blake7: That's harsh, but too true. And I guess the truth hurts.

CrossKrys: Don't get me wrong, B. There are a few cool Christians. But, by and

large, it's a dweeb-fest. I don't
mean to be superficial, but they'd
have more credibility if they wore
better gear and used some
Clearasil—and somebody other
than their moms cut their hair.
Please don't fry me for saying all
this, God, OK? It's just my honest
opinion. And I really hurt for these
poor Herbs sometimes.

God: I have never feared honesty. But,
Krys, you must understand that
outward appearances don't influence
Me. I am concerned about the
condition of the soul, not the
condition—or color—of the skin.
And I want you to think deeply
about what you have been saying:
Why do you think so many
outcasts, social misfits, and those
deemed unattractive by the latest
magazine-cover standards turn to
Me? Perhaps they realize more than

others their need for Me. The so-called cool ones, perhaps they feel no sense of need. Everyone admires them. They get validated every time they look in the mirror; so where's the motivation to look within their souls?

Blake7: Yeah. I think too many people are much more concerned with looking good than being good. And, remember, Krys, Jesus wasn't cool in the sense we define it today. The Bible says he wasn't fine-looking like King David. Hang on, I gotta get my Bible from downstairs. There's something you have to hear.

****

March 31

Private Chat #114:

The Rap on Rep, Version 2.0

 Participants Here: 4
God · Blake7 · CrossKrys · JennSmiles

Blake7: OK, I'm back. Listen to this, from Isaiah 53: "He had no beauty or majesty to attract us to him, nothing in his appearance that we should desire him. He was despised and rejected by men, a man of sorrows, and familiar with suffering."

CrossKrys: Whoa. Every painting I've seen of Jesus depicts him as a movie star-looking dude. And I've never heard the "man of sorrows" thing. Suffering was FAMILIAR to him! I caught that. It's something that was part of his life. Jump back!

195 ↕

Blake7: There's more, Krys: Jesus hung out with society's lowest order of people. He wasn't rich. He didn't have political clout. In the world's eyes, He was born out of wedlock. About all He had was a pair of sandals, a few flaky disciples, and the truth.

JennSmiles: But what about all those paintings and movies and stuff? It's always a handsome leading man who plays Jesus. Are Christian movie-makers and artists just as image-obsessed as the rest of us?

Blake7: It's just human artistic spin control. The Bible totally says that there was NOTHING about Jesus' appearance that attracted people to Him. Think about it, guys, Jesus was the one Person in human history who could have CHOSEN to be the handsomest, wealthiest, and most powerful Being on the planet. But He deliberately chose to be poor and plain. The Bible quotes Him as saying that He didn't have a place to lay His head. Even foxes have holes, He said, and birds have nests, but all He had were miles of dusty roads to travel.

CrossKrys: I so admire that. I admire anyone who follows his own heart, even if it means sadness. But I have to admit: I'm lonely. I'm not like the other church kids at school. And now I'm not like the rest of the people either. I hate it that I hunger for popularity and acceptance. I wish I were stronger. But I'm not.

JennSmiles: You know, my school is kind of like what you're talking about. Except J. T., this Mr. Everything/Athlete/Scholar/Homecoming King/yada yada yada. He's a devout Christian.

And nobody hassles him. He'd probably turn the other cheek, but no one wants to find out from experience what he'd do after that. He has some guns on him, let me tell you. He is ripped! But most of the others—oh my. They need a l'il clue. Even a hint would help. And they're always on the wrong side of the issues. Christianity has to be the most un-p.c. religion ever created. What's with uptight, stingy, hateful conservatives all being Christians? How come none of my favorite actors or bands are Christians? Why are the cool social leaders all not Christian?

Blake7: I have to disagree with you there, Jenn. Come on, we've talked about how Jesus hung with all the so-called low-lifes of society. And that wasn't just "liberal." It was illegal! Jewish people were forbidden by law from associating with "sinners." Jesus was an original social rebel. And He is the most compassionate Person ever to walk this earth.

CrossKrys: OK, I'm feelin' that. But God, I'm with Jenn on the issues thing. How come Christians always come off sounding shrill, uninformed, and just plain out of touch? Every time Christians go on a show like Politically Incorrect, everybody just puts them down and makes fun of them. Why don't they take a more effective stance—maybe take different positions on issues?

Blake7: I hear what you are saying. Man, I'd love to see, just once, a Christian go on one of those shows and kick butt, religiously speaking, of course. Is that ever going to happen, God?

God: I grow weary of the programs you refer to, weary of the public debates and school board meetings. Everyone shouts. No one listens. And no one learns. Volume is regarded as a substitute for veracity. Whoever speaks most forcefully and garners the most applause is deemed to be right.

Blake7: But aren't we supposed to defend our faith?

God: Yes, My servant Peter writes of that in My Book. But how many Christians truly defend their faith, their hope? Or do they instead defend their political position? Their prejudices? Their theological turf? Blake, what does the poster on your bedroom wall say?

Blake7: That's so weird; I was just looking at it. It's a quote from St. Francis.

It says, "Go into all the world and preach the gospel. If necessary, use words."

God: What if My people lived those words? What if they realized that it is how you treat one another, not what's on your bumper stickers, that matters? Action is the true test of faith. Faith without works is dead. And dead faith does nothing but stink up a place. What if My people dared to live lives of love? Tonight in the world, including the United States, people go to bed hungry. And many don't even have a bed to go to. Tonight, in New York alone, there are more than 10,000 of My children who are homeless. What if My people strived to feed them, to house them?

Blake7: Yeah, it seems like sometimes we are more interested with feeding our egos or our political organizations. Or our media machinery.

God: Recall My Son's words: "By this will all people know that you are My disciples, if you love one another."

Blake7: I am busted on that one, Sir. Sometimes I get so fixed on proving that Christianity is true that I get really hostile toward people. I want to win arguments. And I get defensive when someone dares to suggest I'm uncool. I'm thinking that if I loved more, listened more, and preached less, people would respect it more when I did say something.

JennSmiles: I'm with you on that one, B. It's like a lot of those pro-lifers. They scream and rage at pro-choicers like me. I really feel like they hate me. I remember this one chick getting in my face at school. I could basically taste what she had for lunch. The names she called me . . . it made it hard to believe that she was doing what she was doing because she loves the unborn. All I saw was hate.

Blake7: Busted again. Man, I went off on this girl in a sociology class last year. She hasn't spoken to me since.

CrossKrys: Guys, I'm still struggling on this one. I agree that if people of faith were more loving, their message would be more credible and more attractive. And maybe they would be more accepted by non-believers. But the belief systems are so different; there's always going to be friction. If I follow the Christian road, let's face it: I'm going to be an outcast. And that prospect is a lonely one.

God: You speak the truth. Not many will walk the narrow road that leads to life. But think of those who have walked that road. Paul. Joseph. Peter. St. Francis. Mary, Jesus' earthly mother. Martin Luther. Thomas More. William Wilberforce. You are in good company.

Blake7: Yeah, besides, Krys, think about the whole popularity/public image thing. Think of the pop band that was so "it" last year—but is the object of ridicule this year. And remember who graced the cover of *People's* Most Beautiful list just three years ago? Neither do I. But she's no doubt been replaced by someone younger, more buzz-worthy, and more beautiful by our fickle human standards. And do you follow the approval ratings for the president? They ebb and flow like the tides.

God: Only with a lot less regularity. The tides, you can depend on. Blake, please read for us Ephesians 3:17.

Blake7: I'm on it. Here goes: "May love be the root and foundation of your life."

God: Tonight, as you lie in your beds, think upon those words. Meditate on them. Dream on them. Love: the root of your life, from which all else grows. Love: the foundation upon which all else is built. My Word says of Me, "God is Love."

Blake7: I remember singing "God is love" back in Sunday school. Weird . . . we don't sing it in youth group or church.

God: Yes, weird indeed. I am Love. My Word doesn't say, "God is Law," "God is Doctrine," "God is Punishment." Love defines Me.

And I define love. If you love others, you will share who I am with them.

Blake7: I will try to do that, Sir.

CrossKrys: I will too.

JennSmiles: OK, whatever. It's not like I have anything against love. I'll see what I can do. Maybe I'll at least try to LIKE someone. But right now, I'd LOVE some sleep. I think we all would.

CrossKrys: Oh yeah!

God: Goodnight then. And by the way, I love you all.

****

April 3

Private Chat #115:

Ace—Lost in Space

Participants Here: 4
Blake7 · JennSmiles · CrossKrys · God

Blake7: God, we need Your advice.

God: I am listening.

Blake7: Jenn heard from A.C. this week. He was totally baked, from the sounds of it. Barely coherent. How can we stop him from experimenting with drugs?

JennSmiles: I think he's doing more than experimenting. More like extensive research. He thinks he can keep it under control.

CrossKrys: Yeah, but he doesn't seem to be one of those people who can just use recreationally once in a while and not let it mess up his life.

God: Why do people take drugs?

Blake7: As an escape?

God: Escape from what?

Blake7: Reality? Life, pressure, pain, despair. The horrors of the world.

God: Does it work?

JennSmiles: Temporarily. You don't really get away from your problems. I think it helps some people feel different for a little while until they can deal.

CrossKrys: But drugs make the problems worse.

God: Consider this: What part of your body do drugs affect?

CrossKrys: Your brain. I mean "the brain."

God: And what part of your body do you use to decide if something is a bad idea?

CrossKrys: Your brain! That's weird. I was trying to tell Ace this very thing a while ago!

God: You told him the truth. I gave each of you a body and mind to use while you're on the earth. It's up to you to be good stewards and use them wisely.

JennSmiles: So, it's like they say: our bodies are temples, right?

God: They didn't say that, I did.

Blake7: How come "they" get credit for so many good things that You said, and people blame "the Almighty" for all the dumb things humanity is responsible for?

God: Because My road is the high road. Accepting Me means accepting a different standard. People choose for themselves a way that is much easier to walk. But where does it lead them? Look at A.C. He takes the easy way out, and ultimately, it will cost him.

CrossKrys: Are you saying that there is no hope for him?

God: I am Hope for him. I can save him from drugs or any other danger if he calls on Me. And don't fool yourselves. I am the only true Hope for any of you, whether you are poisoning yourself with chemicals or some other poison such as hatred, deceit, or pride. A.C.'s sickness may be more obvious, but you ALL need a cure.

Blake7: Wow. We galloped in here on our collective high horse ready to look down on poor A.C., and we forgot that without You, we are no better off.

God: I love for you to care about people and to ask Me to help them. Just don't forget to start with your own heart.

****

Private Chat #116:

All for One

Participants Here: 4
God · Blake7 · JennSmiles · CrossKrys

CrossKrys: OK, God, I have quite a conundrum to discuss tonight.

God: I am listening.

CrossKrys: Well, sometimes you talk about Jesus as your son. It's obvious that you love him and are proud of him. But other times, you talk about how YOU walked the earth. It's like sometimes you and Jesus are the same person, and others you are father and son. I don't get it. And don't even get me started on the Holy Spirit. That has come up in youth group a few times. The whole trinity thing gives me major brain cramps.

God: You went fishing with your father last spring.

CrossKrys: Uh . . . disconnect alert. Reeeeeeeeeeee-Reeeeeeeeeeeeee-Reeeeeeeeeeee. (That's my disconnect alarm sound, for those of you who didn't know.) So, anyway, what does that boring fishing trip have to do with how one God can be three people at the same time?

God: What did you see when you looked at the lake?

CrossKrys: Well, no fish jumping, that's for sure. In fact, there were still chunks of ice in the water. Maybe that's why we didn't catch anything. Which raises the question: Where do fish go when the water gets cold?

How do they survive if a lake is totally iced over? Never mind. One conundrum at a time. OK, what did I see? Well, water and ice.

God: And what else?

CrossKrys: I don't know. No other people. They had too much sense to get up at 5 a.m. and freeze their extremities.

God: Remember, Krys. Picture the lake.

CrossKrys: OK, picturing now. Hmmm. Well, when we first got there, there was steam rising off of the water. It looked kinda cool. Oh, yes! I see what you're getting at, Mr. God Sir!

JennSmiles: Wanna share with the rest of us, Ms. Genius?

CrossKrys: Here's the deal: this lake, this same body of water, was three different forms at the same time. It was mostly liquid, but there was also solid ice in the water and steam, a gas, rising FROM the water. One substance, three forms simultaneously.

Blake7: What Krys witnessed was the triple point of water. It's one of the best ways to illustrate how God, Jesus, and the Spirit can be made of the same stuff, yet operate in different forms. It's how God could experience being human.

God: Yes, My Son lived it all. Imagine Him as an infant, shivering and crying from the cold. Imagine Him as a young Boy, afraid of strange, threatening noises in the darkness. Retching and feverish with an illness. Stumbling on a rock and turning His ankle or cracking open His head. He experienced all of that and more, and so did I. Remember,

My Son and I are One, as you have learned today.

CrossKrys: I never thought of that. That is so sad. That Jesus had to endure the same crap we do.

God: How else could My Son and I truly understand your prayers, your frustrations, your lives? And being human is not all pain and sadness. Jesus also knew the pure joy of sprinting across a field with the wind at His back and the morning sun kissing His face. Sitting down to a good meal after a day of hard work. Being hugged and praised by His mother when He completed His chores.

Blake7: I've always admired Jesus for the time He chose to live on this earth. A time with no antibiotics, no air conditioning, and no indoor plumbing.

JennSmiles: No DVDs, no McDonald's either. No Tommy Hilfiger or shampoo and conditioner in one. Let's not forget the really important stuff.

Blake7: I think it would have been hard to survive back in those times, let alone transform the world and stand organized religion on its head.

CrossKrys: Hey, I am wondering: Jesus was a flesh-and-blood person; what kind of guy was he? And I'm talking about his personality, not his teachings, necessarily. Who was he? How did he relate to people?

God: Excellent question. Consider this: He was gentle to the woman at the well, a woman who was promiscuous at a time when it was punishable by death. He also saved the life of another woman caught in adultery.

Blake7: Yeah, that was when He told all those hypocrites, "Let him who is without sin cast the first stone." That totally rocked, no pun intended. He didn't play super hero. He didn't play the martyr and throw himself in front of her. He just spoke a few words of truth, and these bloodthirsty, high-and-mighty hotheads were paralyzed by their own hypocrisy. Then He told the woman that He didn't condemn her. He told her to change her behavior, but He didn't condemn her. I love reading how He asks her, "Where are your accusers?" Heavenly Father, I have to tell You: You have a great Son.

God: Thank you. I think so too.

JennSmiles: So, you're telling me that Jesus actually stood up for a woman who was skanking around? He didn't yell at her later or anything?

Blake7: That's right, Jenn. He befriended women in trouble. He was called a glutton and a drunkard because of the people He chose as friends. You see why you gotta love this Guy? You see why I get excited when I talk about Him? As a kid, I wanted a hero so bad. But sports heroes ended up beating their wives, taking drugs, taking advantage of young girls, demanding more money, dissing the very fans who made them famous. Rock stars sold out—allowed their once-meaningful anthems to be turned into commercial jingles to sell tacos, trucks, or mufflers. And some overdosed. Others just became irrelevant. Movie stars changed spouses about as frequently as they changed their socks. Presidents lied. Then I read about Jesus. And I knew I had found my Hero.

JennSmiles: I have never had a hero, come to think of it.

Blake7: It's not too late.

God: Blake is right.

JennSmiles: Maybe it's not too late in life, but it's definitely too late in the evening. Same time next Friday, gang?

****

Private Chat #117:

Love Jones

Participants Here: 4
JennSmiles · God · Blake7 · CrossKrys

JennSmiles: God, I'm so glad you're here.

God: I, also, am glad I am here.

JennSmiles: Well, I don't know if you'll stay glad. Because I've been thinking a ton about love. Love and forgiveness, to be exact. And something's not making sense.

Blake7: I am eager to hear this, Jenn. I get a sense you have really been "pondering" lately.

JennSmiles: That I have. You know I had that meltdown . . .

221

CrossKrys: Meltdown? Sorry, Jenn, I'm drawing a blank here. What meltdown?

JennSmiles: Oh, my sides. They are literally aching with laughter. Please stop, you're gonna make me chuckle so hard I'll bust a rib. But seriously, I know you have all been like, "We forgive you, Jenn." But it doesn't work for me, in one case. In God's case.

God: Why do you feel that way?

JennSmiles: It's like I said that night: I'm a bad seed. You know, I lied about so many things—the virgin thing, the divorce thing, and so on. But I didn't truly FEEL bad until that night when Krys spilled her guts. I should have stepped in that night and stood by you, K. I know that's what you would do for me. But, NO, I left you hanging and humiliated. What kind of person does that to a friend?

CrossKrys: It's OK, Jenn, you said you were sorry. That's the end of it.

JennSmiles: No, it's not. You are an angel, but that doesn't change who I am. I escaped your wrath. But I can't escape from who I am.

Blake7: I think you are looking at this the wrong way, Jenn. It's not about you. It's about God. I'm looking at Luke's gospel in my Bible right now. Jesus tells of this son who demands his inheritance from his father; then he books. He thinks he's mad cool. He drinks. He womanizes. Then he runs out of benjamins, and the party's over. His party posse deserts him. He probably goes through withdrawal from the ancient equivalent of Jack

Daniels. And he probably has a raging case of VD to boot. He has to take a job feeding pigs.

CrossKrys: Oooh. My uncle has pigs. It's not a pretty sight at feeding time—or any other time, for that matter. And the smell is horrible. It stays in your nose for days.

Blake7: Oink and amen to that. And here's the key part, Jenn. The son doesn't feel a bit of remorse until the money and liquor vanish and the hotties say adios and go in search of another sugar daddy. Only then does he come to his senses. He decides he'll go back to his father, grovel for a while, and maybe get back in the old man's good graces as a hired hand.

JennSmiles: So, did his dad take him back as a worker? I think I'd slam the door right in his face.

Blake7: Then you gotta hear this! Listen: This poor sap heads home, and while he is still A LONG WAY OFF, the father sees him. Comprende? His dad is watching for him. He's straining his eyes every day in hopes that his son will return. And on this particular day, the father sees his son. And he's not filled with rage or I-told-you-so self-righteousness. He's filled with compassion. He runs to his son. He sprints for him, just like I do the last lap of the mile. He throws his arms around him and kisses him.

CrossKrys: Jump back!

Blake7: Jump way back! Then the father throws this party for his wayward son. He gives him a robe, a symbol of distinction. A signet ring, which gives him authority. And sandals, which symbolize freedom. You see, servants didn't wear sandals in those days. It helped discourage them from running away. Then they kill a fattened calf, and it's this major celebration for everybody. Except the calf.

JennSmiles: I don't see why the father was so nice. The son didn't deserve any of that.

Blake7: And that's the point. He didn't deserve it. We don't deserve God's love and forgiveness. But we get it because it is pure love. Pure grace and kindness.

JennSmiles: So that father in the story is like you, God?

God: Not "like Me." I AM that father. I watch for My children to come home. I don't sit behind closed doors and wait for a knock. And when you are still a long way off, I run to you. I don't wait for you to run to Me. And in the story Blake just shared, the father hugged and kissed his son before he heard any explanation or apology. You see, it's not why you come back that's important. It's not where you have been. The prodigal son didn't return to his father until all his other options dried up. He chose to feed pigs before he thought of going to his father. But he discovered that what the father wants—what I want—is for My children to be home with Me. Come home, Jenn. I am watching down the road for you.

Blake7: Please, Jenn.

CrossKrys: Guys, I think she's gone again. Why does she always bail at the worst times?

Blake7: Aw, man. This is so frustrating! What is with her?

God: Peace. Be still. She is not gone. She is talking to Me now.

CrossKrys: I don't see anything? Is she sending you an IM or something?

God: In a manner of speaking, yes. It's called prayer.

CrossKrys: Jenn—praying? Will wonders never cease?

God: No, they won't.

****

Private Chat #118:

Fond Farewells

 Participants Here: 3
JennSmiles · CrossKrys · Blake7

CrossKrys: I hate this.

JennSmiles: I'll second that emotion. Blake, Krys, you freaks. Why are you doing this to me?

Blake7: I'm sorry, guys. I'm going to miss this. I'm going to miss you both.

JennSmiles: Ditto that, B. You really going to be away from your 'puter for the whole summer though?

Blake7: Pretty much. I've always wanted to bike across the country. Now is the time. Then when I get back, there's

229

this track camp up north. I don't
want to get smoked at regionals like
I did this season. I've got to bring
my mile time way down if I want
to run with the big dogs.

JennSmiles: Well, I guess I can respect that. But,
you, Krys, are you sure that you
won't be online this summer?

CrossKrys: Doubtful, but not hopeless. I'm
spending the summer in Montana
with Biological Mom. She's an
avowed technophobe. But I imagine
I might make some friends who can
hook me up. Don't be surprised if I
pop up on your screen sometime.

JennSmiles: Thank God for that.

CrossKrys: Speaking of the deity—I wonder why
he's not chatting right now. Maybe
he wants to give us some time.

JennSmiles: Yeah. And speaking of missing persons, I have not heard a l'il peep from Ace in a long time. I got this long, rambling, incoherent e-mail a while back. He was still trying to justify using drugs and stuff, but his stance was rather feckless.

CrossKrys: Feckless? Nice word.

JennSmiles: Yep. I'm still on that new-word-a-day thing. Pretty impressive, huh?

CrossKrys: Do you know what feckless means, exactly?

JennSmiles: Sure . . . uh, it means that something lacks feck. Did I use it wrong?

CrossKrys: Nah, you're good.

JennSmiles: Thanks. You're good too.

Blake7: Hey, girls, I'd like you to meet someone. Lorri (a.k.a. Strider 77) is

my little sister. She's going to
keep my computer warm for me
while I'm gone. She's been wanting
to meet you, so I figured now is
the time.

Strider 77: Hey.

CrossKrys: Hey right back.

JennSmiles: It's a pleasure, Lorri. Blake, you
never even told me you had a sister.
It's weird; we've been friends the
whole year, and you know
everything about Krys and me. But
we know very little about you.

Blake7: Maybe that will change when I
return.

CrossKrys: It better. So, Lorri, how old
are you?

Strider77: Thirteen. You?

CrossKrys: Sixteen.

JennSmiles: I'm eighteen, but I've been eighteen since I was thirteen, really.

Strider77: I've been thirteen since March 23.

JennSmiles: Well, it will be nice to have someone to keep me company, since all my other friends are DESERTING ME.

God: Not everyone is deserting you.

JennSmiles: You are here! Yes! I'd say, "Long time, no talk," but we've been talking almost every night lately.

God: Yes, we have.

Blake7: Jenn, I can't tell you how happy I am.

JennSmiles: Well, don't get too happy, Blake-o. You don't hear what I say sometimes. I think God and I are going to have one of those stormy relationships.

And stormy is a fitting word. Because that's what my life is. Parents fighting around me, guys hassling me, teachers pressuring me to go to college. Any chance of calming things down for me God?

God: You carried your niece into your house last week because it was pouring outside. You wrapped your jacket around her and used your body to shield her from the storm.

JennSmiles: Why do I get the impression that there's a lesson coming here?

God: You are right. If you could have seen your niece's face as she nestled close to you, you would have seen peace in her eyes. She knew that a storm was raging around her. But she was warm, safe, and dry in your arms. That's the way it is with Me. Sometimes I will calm the storms.

But other times, I will let them rage
and calm My children instead.

JennSmiles: I used to have nothing to hold on
to during life's, uh, storms. Now
perhaps I do.

Blake7: What about you, Krys? What
effect has this past year of chats
had on you?

CrossKrys: You mean other than the fact that
I've met friends I never want to
lose? Or that I've spoken to God
live and in person? Sometimes I
wake up from a dead sleep and say
to myself, "Oh, my, I've met God!"
How cool is that? It's weird—I
came up with my screen name
because I am a big-time cross-
country skier. But now the "cross"
part has a different meaning to me.

JennSmiles: Well, I hate to break up this little
happy-fest, but the fact is that we

are going somewhat separate ways now, and I'm going to miss my friends. God, will you chat online with me anymore, with us anymore?

God: I am always talking to My children.

JennSmiles: What do you mean? I'm afraid of losing this. Of losing touch.

God: Blake, would you get your Bible for us? You left it on the TV.

Blake7: OK, BRB.

****

Private Chat #118:

Fond Farewells, Version 2.0

Participants Here: 5
Strider77 · Blake7 · God · CrossKrys · JennSmiles

Blake7: I'm back with Bible in hand.

God: Please read Isaiah 41:10. What do I say there?

Blake7: "Do not fear, for I am with you; do not be dismayed, for I am your God. I will strengthen you and help you; I will uphold you with my righteous right hand."

JennSmiles: But how will you do that? How can you be with me if I can't find you in a Private Chat anymore?

God: Watch and see. Those who seek Me find Me. Whether they have a computer is not relevant. I will never leave you. Remember that.

Blake7: Jenn, we have an entire Book that is God's ongoing message to us. We have pastors, artists, musicians, teachers. And David said that his own heart instructed him. So listen to God's messengers. And listen to your heart.

JennSmiles: I will do that. Since I have been drawing closer to God, it's like my heart has been telling me some cool stuff. I don't feel so tossed around like a rag doll in a rottweiler's mouth anymore. But, still, what am I going to do without you guys? Without these times?

CrossKrys: Well, Jenn, my friend, we have talked about life over the past year.

Maybe it's time to log off and start LIVING it.

God: An excellent idea, Krys. Life is worth living big. I want you to have life, and have it abundantly. I am not the Great Denier, as some have said. I am the Great Giver. I give you freedom. And I give you wisdom so that you may fully and purely enjoy that freedom, not abuse or squander it.

JennSmiles: This may sound dumb, but can we really be happy and not feel guilty about it? We don't have to be all dour and sour—or red-faced and pompous like some of those TV preachers?

God: Be happy, young friends. Let your hearts give you joy in the days of your youth. May you know always what your life is worth. This is your time. Drink life in. Breathe it in. Create something beautiful. Love someone unlovable. Say something bold and true. Give. Forgive. Sing. Revolutionize your world for good.

JennSmiles: I will try. But you've got my back, right, God?

God: I do. I will sustain you. You will experience trouble in this world. But take heart, I have overcome the world. Difficult people, difficult times, they are not your enemy. They are your opportunity! And remember, I am with you always. I am watching over you, with love and hope. I, My holy angels, and all the heroes of the faith. We cheer you on. My angels celebrated for all they were worth when I saw you from the road, heading for home.

JennSmiles: That is mad cool.

CrossKrys: So, God, is this really it for you and the chat rooms?

God: You will always be able to find Me. If not here, then somewhere else.

Blake7: Sir, would Jesus ever visit us in the chats, as You did?

God: All things are possible.

Blake7: . . . even finding the will to say goodbye to my friends. I have to get my bike to the shop for a tune-up. And the shop closes soon. Krys, Jenn, I will write to you whenever I can. I will think of you. I will pray for you. And let's all pray for Ace. We can't forget him. Anyway, thank you for inviting me into your world.

JennSmiles: You better write, B. And maybe we can go to that church camp next summer, the one you e-mailed me about?

CrossKrys: Yeah, maybe we can all go. Well, I may have a 4.0, but I'm lousy at goodbyes. So I'll just say I love you all. And, Blake, I promise I'll try to find a church in Biological Mom's town. And if I charm my way into some computer-owning girl's life, you and I can carry on just like old times, Jenn. And we can get to know you, Blake's Little Sister.

Strider77: I'm looking forward to that.

JennSmiles: OK, before we all get weepy, let's wrap this up. We've said what needs to be said. So, I'm gonna count to three, then we do the simultaneous log-off and shut-down, OK?

Blake7: OK, but I have a little benediction to pronounce as we go: Now may

the Lord bless you and keep
you . . .

JennSmiles: One . . .

Blake7:   . . . and make His face shine upon
you and be gracious to you . . .

JennSmiles: Two . . .

Blake7:   . . . and turn His face toward you
and give you peace.

God: Amen.

JennSmiles: Three!

****

Epilogue
Private Chat #119:

What Now?

Participants Here: 2
Strider77 · JennSmiles

JennSmiles: So, tell me, kid, are you anything like your brother?

Strider77: Well, not really. First, he's a guy, of course, and he's a lot faster than I am. But someday, I'm gonna smoke him like a Christmas ham.

JennSmiles: Are you as much a person of faith as he is?

Strider77: Let's not go there. That's kind of a sore subject for me. See, our parents FORCE me to go to church, and I hate it. But Blake goes because he wants to, so that makes me look really sorry by comparison. It's like Good Kid/Bad Kid. I'm tired of the unfavorable comparisons. I'm tired of living in his shadow. You know, sometimes I think of doing something really nasty just to show my parents how un-Blake-like I am.

JennSmiles: Do you believe in God, Lorri?

Strider77: You know, my parents don't even ask me that question. They just assume I do. And I don't know if I believe. I call myself a Christian, just like I call myself a Randall (that's our last name, in case you didn't know). It's like I inherited my name and my religion at birth. I never got a say in anything. I don't know. I guess I don't really believe God has much interest in someone like me. I'm just a kid with this bigger-than-life Super Brother whose goal is to save all of humanity. How do I deal with that? I'm just a confused kid who has no clue about life, to be honest.

JennSmiles: ☺

Strider77: You find all this funny?

JennSmiles: No, not at all. It's just that I relate to you so much. And I'm just sitting here thinking, Whoa, do this girl and I have a LOT to talk about!

Strider77: OK, but don't think you're gonna flip me to being all religious like Blake. That's not who I am.

JennSmiles: I won't try to flip you. But if it happens, it happens. I didn't think it would ever happen to me. But I flipped like a pancake. I heard this story about this father running down the road to love on his son . . . I need to tell you that story. I'm sure you've heard it before, but maybe you've never really heard it, know what I mean? I need to tell you lots of stuff. And I will listen to you too. I will do nothing but listen, if that's what you need on some particular day. Deal?

Strider77: That's cool with me. Do you think God or Jesus will join us sometime?

JennSmiles: Maybe. But let's just become friends and see what happens. After what I've seen this past year, who knows whose name might pop up on the screen someday. . . .

Glossary of Internet Terms and Teen Vernacular

A/L = Age/Location. One of the first bits of information shared by Internet chatters.

A/S/L = Age/Sex/Location.

Amped = Excited, enthusiastic (e.g., "I am so amped about having tacos for dinner tonight!")

Baked (or Budded) = Under the influence of marijuana.

Bank = Something or someone that is trustworthy and reliable. As in "You are bank!"

Benjamins = Large sums of money (so named for Benjamin Franklin, whose distinguished countenance graces the $100 bill).

Big ups (to you) = A term of commendation or compliment (e.g., "Big ups to you for giving me $100 in cash for my birthday!")

Biznitch = A cranky, disagreeable person.

Blunt = To put it bluntly, a blunt is a cigarette containing marijuana.

BRB = Short for "Be right back."

BTW = Short for "By the way."

Butch (verb) = To destroy, to kill in a violent manner (e.g., "While driving to school today, I accidentally butched a squirrel that was trying to cross the road.")

Calling smoke = Serving notice that you know someone is being dishonest, disingenuous, or evasive.

Gat = Street slang for a handgun.

Ghetto (adjective) = Characteristic of a rough, street-wise, and criminal lifestyle (e.g., "That hip-hop artist is trying to look very ghetto, but he's actually a rich guy from Carmel.")

(To) Go PBS = To speak in academic, multi-syllabic jargon.

Herb (pronounced with a hard H) = The 21st-century equivalent of a nerd.

IM = Instant Message. Internet chat participants can converse one-on-one via message boxes. Once a message is typed on the screen and sent, it appears instantaneously on the addressee's computer screen.

J/K = Just kidding.

LOL = Laughing Out Loud. This acronym is used to acknowledge a good joke or quip.

Mad cool = Extremely cool. Also, mad bank, mad rich, etc.

Mad-dog (verb) = To hassle or attack someone verbally. To harangue. (Note: It's not mad cool to mad-dog someone.)

Mook = A person characterized by raunchy language and a preoccupation with sex. (This term should not be confused with "Mookie," a moniker for several fine baseball players, such as Mookie Wilson.)

Narc (verb) = To report illegal activities to parental or legal authorities (e.g., "My sister narc'd on me because I had a methamphetamine lab in our basement.")

Playa = One who plays the field, has many romantic partners, and avoids committed relationships.

Ripped = In great physical condition with well-defined muscles.

ROFL = Rolling on the Floor Laughing. (See LOL; then multiply the humor by a factor of 2.3.)

Scoopage = The hottest, late-breaking news.

What's the what? = What, pray-tell, is the problem, the latest news, etc.?

Zig-Zag = A brand of rolling paper used to fashion home-made cigarettes or joints.

About the Authors

Jedd Hafer is a stand-up comic and youth speaker who works nationally. A finalist in the "Tonight Show with Jay Leno Comedy Challenge," he is also a two-time winner of the Colorado Young Writers award. A  piece titled "Overheard At an Amy Grant Concert," which he wrote with his brother Todd, was chosen for the book *The Best Christian Writing 2000.* Jedd's day job is site director at The Children's Ark, a home for troubled teens.

Todd Hafer is editorial director for Hallmark Inc.'s book division. He also tackles a variety of writing assignments for newspapers and magazines. He has won several national and international writing awards, a few of which his children haven't colored on or used to play army. *In the Chat Room with God* is his sixteenth book.

E-mail Todd and Jedd in care of
info@riveroakpublishing.com.

Additional copies of this book and other titles by RiverOak Publishing are available from your local bookstore.

Snickers From the Front Pew

If you have enjoyed this book, or it has impacted your life, we would like to hear from you.

Please contact us at:

RiverOak Publishing
Department E
P.O. Box 700143
Tulsa, Oklahoma 74170-0143

Or by e-mail at: info@riveroakpublishing.com

Visit our website at: www.riveroakpublishing.com